~~SHOULD~~
~~WOULD~~
~~COULD~~
DID.

AMY COUTIN

CONTENTS

To everyone I have met on my adventures and travels, thank you for unknowingly contributing to my amazing stories and memories.
I will truly treasure them forever.

Thank you to everyone I served in the Royal Air Force (RAF) with. Because of you, I always have something to look back and laugh at.
I will always be one of the lads.

Thank you to all my family, but especially my Mum and Dad, for always supporting my spontaneous way of life.

Thank you to Aaron for always believing in me and for always pushing me to achieve my goals. Even though you are a new chapter in my crazy little life, you're part of the story now, and I want you in it till the end.

1 WILD BEFORE I WAS WILD
"If we really love ourselves, everything in life works."

Tuesday, October 3rd, 1989.
Margaret Thatcher was the UK prime minister, 'Ride on Time' by Black Box, was in the top five, and in Milton Keynes hospital, a little blonde, libra legend was being born into this crazy World.
Me.
With the umbilical cord wrapped around my neck, I didn't exactly come out kicking and screaming; in fact, I was blue and basically dead.
I may have even been dead. I'm not quite sure.
I was clearly a big attention seeker right from the moment I popped out.
Anything to have even more eyes on me.
And possibly why I am such a life lover.

I grew up in a pretty, little Oxfordshire village, just outside Bicester, with my mum, dad, younger sister, and a household full of pets.
There was Snaffles the pony (ok, so he didn't actually live in the house, but he was a pet!) Arnie the border collie, Sweep the cat, Midnight the rabbit, Monty and

Feathers the finches, and a tank full of goldfish.

The finches didn't last long. My dad was cleaning the cage out one day, and 'they just flew away'.
Debatable.
I think Dad freed them into the wild, so he didn't have to listen to their birdsong every day, where they probably lasted less than an hour before getting eaten by a cat.

I was brought up in an environment where I was told I could be anything I wanted to be if I just tried.
From a very young age, I wanted to be a pilot or a vet.
I was forever finding birds and animals and taking them home to 'nurse'.
Baby pheasants, pigeons, hedgehogs, I even wrapped up an injured woodpecker and cradled him all the way home. However, they have tiny hearts, and the poor little thing had a heart attack on the way home.
I cried for days over Woody, and knowing my luck, I was probably the one that gave him the heart attack.

When I wasn't trying to mend animals, I was climbing lamp posts, playing knock-knock-run, or sat in the park with the other children in my village.
There was a whole bunch of us.
Girls and boys.
One of which I still stay in touch with, almost 30 years later.
I have fond memories of visiting her house for tea and eating potato smiley faces, beans, and sausages, before going up to Brownies together.
Those were the days.

I look at a potato now and instantly gain a stone.

I was a Rainbow, then a Brownie, and then a Girl Guide. I loved being outdoors and craved doing anything active or skill-based.
I would, and still will, always give anything a go.
We didn't have iPads, Facebook, or PlayStations back then. We didn't even have mobile phones.
We weren't spending hours glued to a screen every day. We were exploring nature, having fun with the bare minimum, living completely carefree.
Drinking from hose pipes, crawling around in mud, just generally not giving a shit about anything.
Like children should when they are growing up.

I was the middle sibling between my two older half-brothers, Stuart and Gary, and my younger sister, Anna.
I quickly learnt that to get along in life, I must do what the boys did.
Or do it even better.
To this day, and throughout everything I have done in life, I have stuck to believing this.
If a guy can do it, I can, and I will, and I'll do it to an even higher standard, or at least try to.

I was fairly sporty in my early years, and I was competitive and determined.
Whether I was riding a horse around an indoor school, doing laps in the swimming pool, prancing around on a balancing beam at gymnastics, or running around the tracks in the playing field.
I wanted to win.
I wanted to stand out.

I wanted to be respected.

Nothing's changed there.

I still have all my medals and certificates, unnecessarily taking up space in the loft, along with everything else I hoard.

Seriously, why do we hold on to so much crap?

Just yesterday, I found a whole bag of birthday cards from over the last 20 odd years, because yeah, they might come in handy one day.

No, no, they won't.

Into the recycling bin they went.

Despite being above average in the athletics department, I completely failed P.E in my GCSEs.

Not because I didn't give it my all, but because I didn't give it anything.

I walked out of the exam.

In actual fact, I told my teacher to 'fuck off', then literally ran off the astroturf and into the changing rooms, crying.

That morning, like any other morning, I was sat by the radiator on the landing of our three-story house, getting ready for another GCSE exam day at school.

Don't ask me why I sat there. I don't know, but it was my 'go-to' spot, my safe place.

Then the phone rang.

It was early, really early, and the phone never rang at that time of day.

Dad didn't even call that early. He worked on the market stalls, so he was up at 4 am most days but never called until at least 8 am.

That was the phone call that changed everything.

That's the moment that I found out my brother had

passed away in the night.

It was over 14 years ago now, but it's still one of those days that sits so vividly in my mind.

I remember how angry I initially was. I kept screaming at Mum, telling her that she was lying, and asking why she would say something so horrible.

Gary wasn't even 25 years old.

He had his whole life ahead of him and yet was taken so cruelly away from us.

He suffered from epilepsy, and although his fits weren't usually severe or very regular, this one cost him his life. He choked on his tongue in his sleep.

Today there are so many drugs and products that help with epilepsy; why couldn't they have been around then?

Gary is the reason why I tell everyone, and I am telling you right now, live your bloody life to the absolute max, don't wait, don't put things off, if you want to do something, just do it, you really don't know what is around the corner, live every single day like it's your last, don't hold grudges, don't wait for that supposedly right moment, don't let work and money ruin your life.

When we are forced into doing something, suddenly the time is there, which means it's there all the time, but we've chosen to limit ourselves by believing it isn't.

If your boss gave you six months to complete a project, it would take you six months, and if they gave you the same project but a week to do it, it would take you just a week, see what I'm saying?

So, stop talking about how busy you are, get the jobs done, but then focus on what you enjoy, instead of feeling weighed down by work and chores all the time.

Live.

Don't just exist.

Have a story to tell, have adventures to share, have experiences to fill your heart and soul, and most importantly, love with every ounce of your body, and tell the people you love that you love them. You never know when it will be the last time.

I was just 16 years old at the time of my brother's death.

Obviously, events like that affect everyone differently.

I physically collapsed at the funeral.

I couldn't cope with it.

As soon as I saw the coffin being carried out of the hearse, I froze, then I fell to the floor and completely broke down.

It was that moment that I knew he really was gone forever; that exact moment hit me like a thousand knives in my heart.

I couldn't breathe, I couldn't stand, I couldn't even talk.

I have never cried so many tears.

I don't remember much of that day after that, apart from the music.

Anna and I chose the funeral songs.

Enrique Iglesias 'Hero' and Atomic Kitten 'Whole again' being some of them.

The most fitting song and one we all remember Gary by today is 'My Way' by Frank Sinatra.

Gary did things his way, that's for sure, he lived a very colourful life, and he loved a drink. I wish I got the chance to have one with him.

He would have been hilarious on a night out.

Gary also loved Eminem, but we didn't really feel it would be appropriated to blare out 'Slim shady', 'Bitch please', or 'Kill you' at his funeral.

I wrote a poem a few days after he died, which he still has with him:

In my heart, the sharpest pain,
The darkest clouds up in my brain,
Just the memories aren't enough,
Yet I know, for you, I will be tough,
I put a star up in the universe,
I still can't believe I have to see you in a hearse,
Why did this have to happen? I just don't know,
Why was it your turn to go?
I will remember the good times, maybe the bad,
I promise for you, I'll try not to be sad,
I will try not to cry,
But it's so, so hard, as I guess this is my final goodbye.

Just a couple of weeks after the funeral, my grandad (my mum's dad), and my pet rabbit passed away.

I felt like we were cursed as a family.

All this heartbreak in the space of just a month.

From that day forward, I began to firmly believe that everything happens in threes.

It's a cruel world at times.

I was in denial for a long, long time and couldn't understand why it had happened.

I never spoke to anyone about it, I refused

counselling, and instead, I became a very angry, selfish individual. I was so angry at the whole World.
I resented everything and everyone.

When we physically hurt ourselves, we are immediately proactive at finding a way to eliminate the pain, right? But when it comes to emotional pain, we seem game for seeing how much torture we can endure and prolong the misery by holding onto our feelings and dealing with it all in our little chaotic heads.
We cause ourselves more and more pain by constantly repeating this ridiculous process.

I repeatedly drowned my sorrows away with alcohol and a lot of it.
I even gave myself gum disease at one point.
What was talking going to do? I wasn't interested in anybody trying to help me. I'd deal with it in my own messed-up way.
Alcohol actually fuelled a lot of my actions, I was a late bloomer and didn't lose my virginity until almost 17, but when I did, it was to my, then, boyfriend's best friend.
Oops, a daisy, but I was just too drunk to care about the consequences.
It wasn't a serious relationship anyway.
I quickly made up for popping my cherry late.
Within two weeks, I'd been with three other men and a girl.
What? Come on, don't judge me. We all must have experiences when we were young, free, and single.
Sorry, Mum, if you are reading this, but you know I had a wild few years. At least I never turned to

smoking or doing drugs, though, right?

I moved in with a friend, Zoe, when I was 18, and that's when my wild partying years truly began.
We were out on the town at least three days a week, and the nights we weren't in town, we would drink and have parties at home or have men over.
Usually, our good friends, Dan and Paddy, our drinking game buddies.
I bloody miss those guys. We had such a laugh. Some of the photos from back then are hilarious.

We would live off beans on toast, wine, malibu, and vodka.
We just didn't care.
We didn't care at all.
At one point, we had over 100 empty bottles in the kitchen.
I have photographic proof, as this was a proud moment for us back then.
We had a big blow-up penis out the front of our house and random road signs in the garden that we had acquired on drunk walks home.
I don't know how we didn't get kicked out, to be honest.
Looking back, I think we were both borderline alcoholics and sexaholics. Still, at the time, we just thought we were living our best lives when really, we were destroying ourselves.

We used to get dressed up in fancy dress just for the hell of it and head out, and it didn't matter what time it was, what day of the week it was, or what time of the year it was. We just did what we wanted to do.

We both must have had at least ten fancy dress costumes, and not the big, ugly, bulky kind but the kinky, barely there, underwear, kind.

One bitter winter evening, we dressed up in our sexy Ann Summers sailors' outfits, that hardly covered our bums, painted our rented house's garage – which we weren't allowed to do, danced our way down to Wetherspoons, got more pissed, caused a scene, broke a few of the towns plant pots, then passed out while playing on the swings in a local park on our drunken walk back home.

Don't get me wrong, they were some amazing years. I had some of the best times while living it up in Birmingham, Bournemouth, Essex, Ibiza, Marbella, but I also lost a lot of friends.

As I said before, I turned selfish and quickly grew fond of men in uniform.

There was a local Army base, so the pubs were full of squaddies.

I was in my element.

On nights out, I would go off and do my own thing, completely abandoning the friend or friends I went out with. As long as I was happy and having a good time, I truly didn't care about anything else.

It was all about me.

I would wear the sluttiest of dresses, I would get men to buy me drinks, I would flirt, I would linger, I would make sure that I rarely spent a penny while I was out, and if I didn't pull, I would sulk, then move on to find someone else.

It was bad; sometimes, I would end up with a guy and just go to a car park, alley, or pub toilet. One time was in a pub kitchen.

It was my distraction, and I loved the thrill of being caught.
My way of blocking out the real world and the sober life I would wake up to in the mornings.
Incredibly sad and desperate, but that is how it was, and that is how I lived my life for a good couple of years.

I wasn't proud of any of it, and I'm not now, but it's possible for anyone to turn their lives around completely — however shitty the circumstance and whatever crap they end up getting themselves into.
The people you surround yourself with are excellent mirrors for who you are and how much, or how little, you love yourself.
I didn't love myself back then, and I didn't feel anything. I just did everything I could to feel wanted and loved by others, by men, when none of it was love at all.

It takes a long time to love yourself. Some people never do. Some people go their whole lives without loving and respecting themselves, but trust me, your life improves dramatically when you learn how to.
You won't be perfect or flawless because nobody is, and that's not what self-love is about.
You just need to realise how valuable and important you are and worthy of happiness.
Self-love is important to living well, but it isn't something you can obtain through a beauty makeover, a new set of clothes, or a fresh relationship.
It comes when you stop comparing yourself to others, learn to be more mindful, and do things solely for

yourself without giving a crap about what others think.

In my early 20's, I settled down slightly and started to pull my life back together. I graduated from college after studying uniformed public services for two years, then started working full time at a local health club complex in Bicester.
However, college was messy.
I don't know how I passed the course, to be honest.
A group of us used to hit the pubs on lunch breaks then take the afternoon lessons half cut.
They were some good years though, we were all close as a group of friends and spent a lot of time together, mainly drinking. The house parties were insane.
Thirteen years later, and we still meet up for reunions.
I love my college crew like I love my family.

At the health club, I became good friends with all the beauticians who worked there and even better friends with a few gym lads.
I have always got on better with males than females, less bitchy.
Dave and Dean became some of my closest male mates. Even now, I would still count them as good friends, especially Dean, who is one of my best buddies, despite now living hours apart and rarely seeing each other. Still, I know that if I picked up the phone and needed help or needed anything at all, he would be there for me, no questions asked.
Well, he bloody better be anyway!
We went on holiday to Kos, in Greece, together, and we had the best time, we explored the island on a quad bike, had a mud spa, went to a water park, had

lovely meals, and just relaxed and had a laugh, true proof that a male and female can be the best of friends without there being anything else to it.

Nothing has ever happened between the two of us.

I also fell in love with a ginger personal trainer who worked at the health club, who wasn't single, but whom I started dating, red flag from the get-go, but my story with him, and a hell of a story that is, is in a different part of this book.

So, you have that to look forward to, and if you like Jeremy Kyle, you will love that section.

Get the popcorn ready.

I built up a huge passion for weight training and quickly gained my fitness qualifications.

I trained with Dean most days, and he helped push me to my absolute limits, I was squatting 100kg, and I only weighed 56kg.

My physique changed quickly, I was getting stronger and stronger, and I started to adore my body. I was toned with a lovely squatters' bum and little girly guns.

It didn't take long for others to notice, and I got asked to be a ring girl at a large boxing night event.

I felt pretty privileged.

Centre of attention, in minimal clothing and surrounded by buff boxers while getting paid for it, what more could a girl want?

I jumped at the opportunity.

The atmosphere on the night was incredible, and I felt amazing.

It was packed. Every seat in the room was taken.

There were over 2000 people there that night.
I stepped up into that ring in my tiny black hot pants, black crop top, and stilettos, and I fucking owned it.
I strutted around that ring with my 'round 3' sign like I was the boss of all bosses.
I knew my arse looked epic.
I did have a couple of vodka shots before, you know, to calm the nerves a little bit.
Friends and strangers not only cheering the boxers but cheering me and yelling my name!
'Coots, Coots, Go on Coooouuuttiinn'
Massive confidence boost.
I had the biggest ego ever that evening.

I enjoyed the night and got proper into boxing, which was not a sport I ever thought I would take to.
One lad did get knocked out just a few feet away from me; the ring girls get to sit right at the side of the ring, so close that I got a blood splatter on my shoe.
Lovely.
Luckily, he was ok, but he could have paid to get my stilettos cleaned.

After the fight night, I continued to receive more and more compliments about my body.
It pushed me to train harder and more consistently.
The gym, along with hiking, was my new distraction, my new escape.

I used to do most of my hikes with my beloved border collie, Arnie.
He came everywhere with me and could always keep up, even as he aged more and more and became

partially blind and deaf.

He loved being outdoors, running free through the fields with a tennis ball, or stick hunting in the woods. He wasn't a big fan of cows, though.

On one of his last walks, he managed a whole 14 kilometres, and, unlike me, he still had energy left at the end.

We had Arnie since he was a pup, and he lived into his 90s in dog years, bless him.

It was another extremely sad day when it was his turn to go.

My mum, sister, and I all went to the vet's and stayed with him right until the very end, right until that bright sparkle drained from his big brown eyes.

I still miss that beautiful boy.

Irreplaceable pooch.

Over those years, I learnt that you could come back from anything, no matter how bad it is; it's all about your mindset and how you deal with a situation.

2 DESERT TREKKING TO PETRA

"If you want to live a life you've never lived, you have to do things you've never done."

I was enjoying my early 20's, but I always felt like I was just going through the motions of living my mediocre life with the occasional burst of excitement here and there.

I knew my life was missing something.

I was unfulfilled.

I worked, trained, walked, and went home to watch crap on the television.

Trapped in that monotonous cycle that so many of us are guilty of.

I didn't just need an adventure, I craved an adventure, and I craved it bad.

When I want something, I will act instantly, and I won't wait or think upon it for a while. No, I will impulsively do anything I get the urge to do.

'Hi Mum, yeah, all ok at this end, oh and by the way, I'm going to Jordan to trek across the desert for charity.'

'Amy, what are you talking about? Who are you going there with?'

'Myself, I'll just meet the others at the airport.'

My spontaneous, independent self had emerged.
One evening, I sat with my milky brew, Coronation Street on in the background, browsing the internet, searching for a challenge.
Trek from the Dead Sea to Petra for 'Wellbeing of Women'.
Perfect, I thought, and right there and then, I signed up and began working my way through the kit lists, itinerary and started setting up fundraising activities.
I'd been abroad many times, but I had never travelled or flown alone.
The whole thing got more and more daunting as my departure day got nearer and nearer.
What had I done?
Plus, I still had to raise another £1000.
I was massively excited yet extremely apprehensive.
I spent days on end organising charity cake stalls, fun runs, and raffles while rushing around buying every item of kit that was required.

There were many other women taking part in the trek. Still, I knew nobody, and I knew I was the youngest person participating.
I was 22.
The average age was 40.
My fitness was nothing to worry about. I knew I was physically able to partake in the challenge. It was my mindset I had to try to convince.

'What if I don't pack the right things?'
'What if nobody likes me?'
'What if something happens and I can't contact my family?'
'What if I get ill?'
'Oh my God, will there be snakes?'
'Shit, where will I go to the toilet?'
'How will I wash my hair in the middle of a desert?'

I didn't even know anything about Jordan.
So, I spent a good few hours researching and learning about the place I was hiking across.
I found out that it is also known as Katie Price and regularly appeared in the Daily Star, FHM, the British edition of Playboy, Nuts, Maxim, Loaded, Vogue and Esquire.
Comedian, aren't I? But seriously, when I started googling Jordan, all I got was a face full of boobs.

A few weeks later, on October 29th, 2011, I was at terminal three, Heathrow airport, giving my mum a teary cuddle goodbye before awaiting the six-hour-long flight to Amman, Jordan.
I joined a small group of the 'Girls Get Tough' trekking ladies who were sat having pre-flight coffee, these women soon became my family, and to this day, thanks to social media, we still keep in touch with the odd reunion.
In total, there were 33 of us on the challenge.
I no longer felt nervous.
All I felt was sheer delight and pure excitement.
My first proper adventure of many.
It had begun.

Chatting, giggling, and getting to know one another made the time in the air pass super quickly.

All were participating in the trek for reasons.

It was fascinating listening to some of the girls' stories. Not one of us had the same background. We were all so different, yet all brought together to do this incredible adventure together.

On our first night, we had the luxury of a beautiful hotel, complete with a swimming pool, amazing food, and overlooking the Dead Sea, the lowest point on Earth.

It was bloody boiling.

The sun was glorious, but knowing I would be trekking through the desert just the following day quickly reminded me that I wasn't on holiday, and I wouldn't be lounging around by a pool, tanning it up with a cocktail in my hand.

A girl can dream.

It was lovely being able to relax while wearing a bikini, though, as the following days I was dressed more like Crocodile Dundee, I had the hat and everything.

If you didn't know, the Dead Sea isn't actually a sea; I didn't know this. It's a Salt Lake bordered by Jordan, Israel, and the West Bank.

It is one of the most intriguing natural phenomena on Earth, and I could see why.

Apart from some microorganisms, algae, and a few floating tourists, the lake is completely devoid of life.

There's no seaweed, fish, or any other creatures found in its salty waters.

The waters are supposedly full of healing properties.

According to legend, Cleopatra loved the Dead Sea and used its products as part of her daily beauty regime.

There you are, that's your interesting fact for the day.

I never believed you could float in the waters, but, oh yes, you most definitely can!

A few of the other girls and I lathered ourselves up in some 'Dead Sea mud', which is known to work wonders on your skin, and we raced down to the magical turquoise lake.

I will try anything these days. If somebody told me dog shit would get rid of wrinkles, believe me, I'd slap it all over my face.

It was a strange experience in the lake.

Due to the high salt content, it's impossible to swim, but you can literally just lay back and float.

The human body isn't as dense as saltwater, enabling us to float on top of it.

Amazing, really, and highly soothing.

I was in the middle of this unfamiliar place, surrounded by plains of sand, just floating in a mystical lake while looking at the crazy, perfectly blue skies.

Completely weightless and completely unrestricted.

The following morning our adventure truly commenced.

With thick socks and hiking boots on, backpacks full and bellies satisfied, we said goodbye to civilization, and after a short coach trip to 'Wadi Chudeira', we took our first steps upon the vast expanse of desert.

The trek had begun.

I was beyond excited.

Our local leaders included a young, barefooted boy named 'Jesus', an extremely friendly older male, 'Abdu', and an armed-up security guard. I didn't catch his name. In fact, I don't think I heard him speak for the majority of the trek, but for safety purposes, we were required to have a gunned-up bloke with us at all times.

Not worrying at all.

We also had two darling donkeys join us, and they helped to carry our precious water.

Day one was all about easing ourselves into the challenge and acclimatizing.

We only had a short eight kilometres to travel, which, trust me, was nothing in comparison with some of the other days.

The biblical scenery was incredible.

I had never been anywhere like it before.

The hike took us through a humungous Wadi. Wadi translates as 'dry riverbed', coloured with shades of bright reds, yellows, and oranges.

It felt like I was walking through a kaleidoscope of sunset.

I snapped away with my camera at every opportunity, but no photograph could do it justice, and back then, I didn't have my fancy Nikon DSLR. I only had one of those disposable cameras that you had to take into Boots to get the film developed.

If you don't remember these, just stop reading my book, you're too young, and I'm jealous of your youth.

The trail passed by several Bedouin camps. Bedouins are known as 'Arab nomads', herders of sheep and camels.

The Bedouins were a violent tribe that lived in independent clans that often had blood feuds with one another.

Sounded like delightful people.

A large proportion of male Bedouins have more than one wife.

Greedy buggers, I know.

A gentleman we met informed us he had three wives and ten children, four camels, and a family of goats.

Yet, he lived alone in his self-built tent in the middle of the desert.

We asked no questions and carried on our way.

I was thoroughly intrigued, though.

Approximately three hours later, the team and I reached 'Wadi Feinan', our camping spot for the evening.

I remember the first night in the desert was almost surreal.

I was sat by a roaring campfire, wrapped up in my freshly bought red sleeping bag, drinking Amstel out of a can and laughing with my newly found friends.

Cheryl, Grace, Kelly, and Shella were the only others in the same age bracket as me, all under 30.

We became known as the 'Famous five'.

It couldn't have been a better end to the first day.

I'm not too sure where the beer even appeared from.

I always find it funny how we all seem to struggle drinking eight glasses of water a day, but give us eight bevvies, and it's so dam easy to down those bad boys.

The temperature in the desert drops significantly in the evenings. There is almost always no cloud cover at all, meaning the night skies are incredible to look at but frigging freezing.

Filled with stars and utterly breath-taking, to this day, I had never seen such starry skies as I did that night, other than when I was in New Zealand.

It does mean being bloody cold while trying to sleep, though. I had a hoody, joggers, two pairs of socks, and a hat on under my sleeping bag.

Wouldn't expect that in the desert, eh?

I certainly didn't.

After an alfresco, sunrise breakfast of coffee and eggs, we were soon off hiking the seemingly, lifeless desert again.

The trek began by cutting through small wadis and climbing over steep ridges, with the magnificent Edom mountains looming on the left side of us.

I never thought I would see a massive expanse of sand as beautiful, but to me, it was.

It was never-ending.

The desert I stood in wasn't just a flat area of sand, just like I imagined. Yes, it was barren, dry, and extremely hot, but there were impressive canyons, magnificent mountains, winding valleys, and the bluest skies I had ever seen.

I felt so free.

And I felt even freer when I had to pee behind invisible trees.

We all got to know one another's wild wee positions quite well.

We had 30 kilometres to cover on the second day, only an hour in, and a few of the other ladies were already suffering in the heat.

It certainly was challenging.

There was no shade at all, and the temperature was already at around 35°c.

The pace had dramatically slowed, and the terrain became stonier and harder to walk on.

This is what I signed up for, I thought. I didn't want it to be an easy walk in the park. I wanted to push myself out of my comfort zone and see what my mind and body were truly capable of.

I soon found out my body was extremely capable of providing me with the most painful blisters.

My heels were in agony. Despite breaking the walking boots in and wearing thick socks, my feet were in bits. Luckily almost all of us had plasters, and jeez, did we need them.

Our lunch break came and went. I vividly remember how grateful we all were to be sitting down and resting for an hour in the shade of a dry riverbed. I've never seen boots pulled off feet so quickly or bags launched off backs in the blink of an eye.

We were all exhausted, sweaty, and only halfway.

Grace, one of the 'Famous five' girls, had a severe nosebleed from the heat; luckily, she was ok, but it just proves the effects of the temperature.

Even the poor donkeys began to struggle.

Snakes.

Yeah, the desert isn't completely deprived of life, and Jordan holds a number of highly poisonous ones.

A couple of screams brought everyone to a standstill. A dusty brown 'Coupler snake' was sliding its way between the group.

I don't fear the weird slithering creatures, yet I wasn't

hanging around to see if it was friendly or not.

Almost eight hours after leaving our campsite that morning, we arrived at a beautiful open area between some rolling dunes.

This was camp for the evening.

It was perfect.

I can picture it right now.

We ate and rested, and then myself and a few others raced to the top of one of the dunes, belly-flopped down off the top, and sled all the way to the bottom.

Ladies in their fifties giggling like schoolgirls while emptying sand particles off their big trekking knickers and sports bras.

It was such good fun, all the pain, and fatigue from the day forgotten.

However, ten years later, I am still finding sand in holes I didn't even know existed.

I slept like an absolute log that night.

Day three.

The muscle aches were setting in.

I was the young one, and I had a back and knees like a granny, so God knows how the real oldies were feeling.

Another early rise in an attempt to cover some of the trails before the sun got too hot.

However, the unsociable wake-up call was worth it for the sunrise. The whole sky was covered in fiery colours, canyons, and valleys illuminated with glowing light, and the arid desert awakening with warmth.

Sunset and sunrise are my favourite times of day, always have been, and I reckon they always will be.

After a breakfast of bread, cheese, cake, and a bucket load of coffee, our team of wonderful women was set

for another full day of hiking across the desert.
Cake in the desert, for breakfast, yes, that was a thing.
We needed the sugar boost…

I'm sure some of you are wondering about how and where we went to the toilet or how we washed.
Well, number ones could be done anywhere, number twos required digging a hole, doing your business, and then burning the loo paper, and washing was primarily done with baby wipes and sanitiser unless we were near a water source which we weren't very often.
Dry shampoo is your best friend when being unable to wash your sweaty, greasy, sand-infested hair.
And with little places to hide out of sight, we all got to know each other well while on 'bathroom' visits.
One of the ladies, and a lady I truly adore, who is now one of my many 'aunties' off the trip, Jayne, always looked flawless, I don't know how she did it
There was me, hair like a homeless person and the face of a zombie, but Jayne was there, perfect skin, bright smile contrasted against her dark pink lipstick, and ears decorated with the most beautiful earrings.
Elegant as ever, even in the desert.

Thirteen kilometres, and just over three hours, into our third day of the trek, we reached an official hiking trail that led to a little Bedouin village.
We hadn't seen any other people for a couple of days.
The sun was scorching, and so we spent a couple of hours at the village learning more about the Bedouins' way of life. All sat comfortably in the shaded tents, giving our tired legs a well-deserved rest.
I knew I had already lost weight, as when I sat down,

I no longer had my tiny bit of belly hanging over my shorts.

The tents we sat under were made from sheep and goat hair, spun by the women of the tribe.
The tent cloths were designed so that they can easily be rolled up and moved, suiting the nomadic lifestyle in which they live.
Groups of women have to work together to sew strips of sheep and goat hair to make up the large tent cloth. The tent cloth is woven loosely to allow heat to disperse. The oils in the goat hair act as a natural repellent to water, meaning the inside of the tent always remains dry.
I found this fascinating.

The tents are traditionally divided into a men's and a women's section, and the furnishing is extremely simple, consisting of rags of carpets, mattresses, and, sometimes, pillows.
I think we all took a moment to appreciate how lucky we were in comparison. Even while in the desert, we had better sleep conditions.
The women's section, usually separated from the men's section by a loose curtain, also includes room for food storage and cooking utensils.
This area is for women only, with the exception of the owner of the tent.
The men's section is primarily used for receiving guests, which is a crucial element in Bedouin life.
I couldn't believe that in this day and age, men and women lived separately; for some, that would be an absolute blessing.
I think my partner would even agree.

We departed the village full of local knowledge and aware of all traditions.

It was a very insightful experience.

The remaining seven kilometres continued over mainly flat terrain. A small part of the trail was even blessed with an array of umbrella-looking Acacia trees, providing us with much-needed shade and cooler air.

Later that afternoon, we set up camp in a wide Wadi area.

Another evening meal of chicken and rice, with a side of vegetables.

I was craving a big greasy burger and chips, but to be honest, I was grateful for any food. By the time we reached camp every evening, we were all famished.

I think I even looked at the donkeys and licked my lips at one point.

The toughest, most challenging day of the hike was upon us.

We had all been pre-warned about the steep ledges and sheer drops we were to face on this part of the route.

Twenty-four kilometres and a testing mountain summit stood between us and our next campsite.

We stuffed our shrinking bellies with a variety of food. I had cake, more cake, and jam for breakfast, don't judge me, and began our morning of hiking along the familiar camel and donkey tracks.

The terrain became more and more undulating underfoot, but the scenery was incredibly beautiful.

We had extraordinary views over the red and orange Petra Mountains, including 'Jabal Haroun'.

Prophet Aaron, brother of Moses and Miriam, died in Petra and was buried on Mount Hor, now known as 'Jabal Haroun' (Mount Aaron).

After a slow five kilometres, we vacated the camel tracks and followed the path of 'Nakev Sleisel'.
This is where the hike became tough.
Really tough.
The summit track was more of a narrow ridge.
Honestly, it was no wider than three feet.
There was no barrier to prevent any one of us from falling down the sheer drop.
My belly was doing somersaults.
I'm not afraid of heights; in fact, I really do enjoy a good mountain climb with far-reaching views. However, when I could plummet to my death in a matter of seconds, it's a very different story.
With my back flat against the rocks and a slow side shuffle with the feet, I made it across the ledge while not looking down.
Still to this day, that is one of the most challenging things I have ever done.
Unfortunately, we did lose one of our gorgeous donkeys on the summit track. He lost his footing and slipped down.
Very sad indeed.
I do believe he survived, but another reminder of the true dangers we faced.
I recall writing in my diary 'Scariest experience ever' when I finally arrived at the top of the mountain.
Only 1023 metres high, yet it felt a hell of a lot higher.
There were even a few tears at the top.
Many of us had overcome massive fears.
A proud moment all around.

We sat at the top of that mountain in complete silence, all of us taking in the panoramic views that surrounded us.

After our incredibly scenic lunch, we trekked down the other side and up another incline until we reached 'Mount Quaran', part of the Red Mountains Ridge.
From here, we had stunning views over the Araba valley.
I started feeling really emotional.
I think it was just down to having a day of achievements and the fact that I was bloody knackered and overwhelmed with all the amazing views.
Or maybe I just really, really wanted some chocolate or gin.

After a leisurely lunch, we continued through the Wadi to 'Baidah' (Little Petra).
We were now only a day away from our endpoint.
Like Petra, Little Petra is a Nabataean site, with impressive buildings carved into the walls of the huge sandstone canyons, which are breathtaking to see in person.
As its name suggests, it is much smaller than Petra, consisting of three wider open areas connected by a canyon.
It is part of the Petra Archaeological Park and included in Petra's inscription as a UNESCO World Heritage Site.
We explored the old caves and temples, took hundreds of photos, and then walked another couple of kilometres to our overnight campsite, 'Ras Suleman'.

This was our last night sleeping, under the stars, in the desert. The following day, we were to hike the last 13 kilometres to our hotel in the red rose city of Petra.

So, our last day of the trek arrived, and what a truly magnificent day it was.
One that I will remember forever.
We all had our last desert breakfast, between the dunes, together, sat in a circle reflecting on the last few days.
It honestly felt like I had known these women my whole life, and despite the age differences, they truly had become my very close friends.
Other than the 'famous five' girls, I had grown to love my 'aunties', Jayne, Ali, Denise, Kath, and Sue.
Honestly, those ladies are incredible.
Plus, they all love a good drink.
I haven't seen them for a while now, my last reunion with them was back in 2015, but I know when I see them again, it will feel like the last time was just yesterday.

Waving farewell to our very last desert campsite, we began the day's trek.
All of us were very grateful for the flat terrain.
After a couple of hours, we passed through an incredible valley of sandstone cliffs, veined with shades of reds, purples, and pinks.
The sun exposed the tones of the cliffs in such a dramatic way.
They looked almost surreal.
The temples and monuments of Petra were hewn out of the colourful sandstone.

That's when we knew we weren't too far away from arriving.

Petra, also known as the 'Rose City' and the 'Lost City', was built more than 2000 years ago. It is believed to have been established in 312 BC, making it one of the oldest cities in the whole World.
It is a famous archaeological site
Petra was the capital city of Nabateans, who were ancient southern Arab people that arrived in Jordan around the 6th century BC.
Films such as 'The Mummy Returns' and 'Indiana Jones and the Last Crusade' are the most noteworthy movies that have been filmed in Petra.
It truly is an incredible place.

Another hour of walking on the rocky trail passed, and we arrived at the 'site entrance'.
To enter Petra, you must purchase tickets and embark on a hike through a dim, narrow gorge called the 'Siq', which is around one kilometre long.
It is bound by rocky cliffs on either side, which are around 80 metres high.
Walking through the natural landform was genuinely an extraordinary experience.
It was a lot cooler in the 'Siq'. The pathway twisted and turned through the gorge until an opening appeared.
It was breathtaking.
Through the thin crack of an exit, I had my first glimpse of 'Al Khazneh', also known as 'The Treasury'. The tomb of a Nabatean King.
If you have watched Indiana Jones, you will know which building I am talking about. It looks incredible

on the television, but seeing this ancient structure reveal itself and be so beautifully preserved was an amazing moment.

I had never set my eyes upon such an incredible building.

Once again, no photo or description could do it justice, but I'll try and set the scene for you.

The red rose facade was lit by the blinding sun, a complete contrast to the cool, dark walls of the 'Siq'.

It was almost 40 metres high and intricately decorated with Corinthian capitals, friezes, figures, and other shapes and patterns.

Tourists cannot enter the interior, but the outside is so remarkable, I don't think I could be any more impressed and didn't feel the need to see the inside anyway.

I got informed, after leaving Jordan, that the inside of the 'Treasury' is just a single square chamber with not much to see anyway!

Our group of amazing ladies then continued deeper into the city of Petra.

We reached the 'Outer Siq'.

Here, the narrow walls opened up into a magnificent plain.

The plain was filled with many camels dressed in their colourful saddles and Bedouins in traditional dresses selling trinkets and small handmade items from stalls.

Some young Bedouins were offering camel rides for a small fee.

I had to give it a go.

I'd ridden many things, but never a camel.

Grace, Kelly, and I went on a camel 'hack' together, not the most comfortable of creatures, I have to say, but a fun experience all the same.

The effect of all this activity made me realise that although we were surrounded by ancient ruins in the middle of a desert, Petra remains, today, a living city thriving with life.

We still had quite a bit of walking to do before we could reach our 'finish line'.

The next part of our trek took us up 850 steps to 'Ad Deir', the largest monument in the Lost City, also known as 'the Monastery'.

It took us almost an hour to climb to the top, but wow, it was so worth it, even though my arse and legs were on fire.

The hike up to the Monastery was, without a doubt, one of the most memorable moments for me.

The whole route up was stunning.

I would turn back every so often to wonder at the valley of Petra unfolding behind me. I took as many photos as I could in an attempt to be able to recall these views forever.

You could see for miles.

Some parts of the trail became more adventurous, sometimes cutting under boulders, sometimes turning into steps that were boulders.

A few of the steps were at least 2 feet high. When you're a short-arse, like me, it's quite challenging to step that high, especially when your legs are already knackered and you have the tightest hips in the universe!

'Top of the World, best view in Petra', a sign read, once we completed the final steps.

We followed the hand-drawn arrows, still ascending,

for just a few minutes. Before we knew it, we were having group photos while standing at 'the top of World' overlooking an incredible view of the entire Petra basin, Monastery, and all the surrounding tombs and mountains.

It certainly made the exertion worthwhile.

After retracing our steps back down, we were on the final leg of our charity trek.

This was it!

Hiking into the more modern part of the city, with people everywhere, made the days of seeing no one in the arid desert vanish.

'Petra Palace hotel' supported a massive purple 'Girls Get Tough' banner, which could be seen about a mile down the road.

We had made it.

It was an extremely emotional time for all of us. I cried like a baby, not because the challenge was over, but because I was super proud of myself and everyone else.

Just very overwhelmed and very much looking forward to sleeping in a bed and having a bloody shower.

In total, we raised over £90,000 for the charity 'Wellbeing of women'.

That's a fantastic achievement just in itself.

The next day, our final day in Jordan, was a free day to explore.

Some of us went on an adventure through 'Wadi Rum', while others stayed local.

A few others and I decided to check out the local shops and grab some souvenirs. After, we hit the swimming pool back at the hotel and relaxed in the sun.

It was heaven.

I do not regret my choice at all. It was an amazing feeling to be able to completely chill out and just soak up the sun without being covered in sand and without having hiking boots on.

Our final evening in Jordan was spent having a delicious Gala dinner.

We ate, drank, danced, and laughed a lot.

It was nice to see everyone dressed up.

On the itinerary, we were told to pack one nice outfit, that was why.

'The famous five' headed into the city after the meal. We stopped off in a strange bar, known as a 'hookah bar', which ended with us buying a few rounds of drinks and a couple of shisha bongs.

Apparently, we were 'living the true Jordanian experience'.

Prior to the meal, we got the chance to visit the Turkish baths.

Which was wonderful and funny. We all had to get topless and were childishly laughing at each other's wobbly bits. Jayne said to me, 'at least yours stay in one place when you lie down. Mine flop under my bloody armpits' did make me giggle.

However, the steam rooms in Jordan aren't exactly health and safety-conscious.

I was sat getting all steamed up in the steamiest steam room ever when suddenly my leg was stuck to the heated metal pipe below the wooden seats.

I couldn't believe the excruciating pain shooting through my calf.

I was in agony, skin ripped off, and severe burns. However, I still carried on in the spa and even had a full body massage with my leg in tatters.

'Yeah, I'm fine, doesn't even hurt.'

At the time, I didn't let anyone know how much pain I was in. I wanted them to just enjoy their treatments and relaxation time.
Stupid really.
I wasn't going to let my injury interfere with my evening either.
I got bandaged up, took some painkillers, and enjoyed my night.

I still have a massive, iron-shaped scar on my left calf, the memento of my adventures in Jordan.

3 LIVING THE DREAM, SERVING THE QUEEN

"In order to kick arse, you must first lift up your foot."

Somewhere in the year 2013, I jumped off the crowded stagecoach bus and started slowly wandering down the busy high street in Oxford city centre.

As much as I loved living in a rural area, there was something about the bustling vibes and atmosphere of the city that I thrived off.

I'd only popped in to grab a few bits in Primark and kill some time on an uneventful Saturday afternoon, but somehow, I ended up in the AFCO (Armed Forces Career Office), signing up to join the RAF.

Well, what better way to be surrounded by men in uniform than to be in uniform myself.

A few months prior to this, I went through an incredibly messy breakup with the ginger I mentioned previously, which affected me badly.

I was with him for just under two years, and I honestly thought he was 'the one'.

He was my first true love anyway, and he was also my

best friend.

We instantly had chemistry, despite him already being in a relationship, which soon ended after we met, and we spent as much time together as we could, inside and outside of work.

He would come round to mine and Zoe's place most evenings.

We started renting a place together quite soon into our relationship. I stupidly thought it was the best thing to do and left Zoe in a shitty position; we fell out for months over it.

The boyfriend and I had planned our whole future together, picked out names for our children. He had even looked at engagement rings and, I was informed, that he was preparing to propose.

We were so happy together, or so I thought.

He was a romantic.

I'd frequently come home to candles up the staircase and rose petals on the bed.

He used to leave me cute little love notes everywhere.

He made me feel so special.

We even got matching tattoos.

My heart was so full of love for him.

I completely adored him and the way he made me feel.

My family never really took to him, especially my dad and brother.

They both thought he was an arrogant, cocky bastard.

Which I suppose he was.

He, undeniably, did love himself.

He had an amazing body, and he did work hard for it.

His arms were astounding, but he knew it and used to

show it off a lot.
I do like a good muscular set of arms, massive fan of the guns.

It was Christmas time, and his Father lived over in Prince Edward Island, Canada, so the unnamed boyfriend and I flew out to spend the festive season with his dad and his family.
At least it was another tick off the bucket list as I had never visited America or Canada before.
A few days into our visit, he started being quiet around me, things seemed awkward, but he insisted everything was fine.
I was already starting to feel homesick as I had never spent a Christmas away from my family. Hence, the atmosphere between my partner and me made me stupidly anxious and upset.
I hated it.
I didn't even enjoy Christmas day.

It was Boxing day morning when he admitted to me that he was in love with somebody else.
That somebody else being his married stepsister of all people.
I knew they were close, but it never even crossed my mind that they were THAT close.
Initially, I was just disgusted!
I wanted to be a complete bitch about it and go and tell his whole family the true reason why we were over.
I never did.
I phoned my dad that morning, bawling my eyes out.
I don't think my parents have ever felt so hopeless.
I was over 3000 miles from home and over eight

hours away on a plane, well, two planes, actually.

At that moment, I was feeling my most alone.

Completely lost.

All I wanted to do was go home and have a big cuddle from my mum.

And believe me, I tried.

But, due to the horrendous snowstorms we had been encountering, I couldn't get a flight for another ten days!

Those remaining days and hours in Canada were absolute torture.

I wouldn't wish anything like that upon anyone.

I was stuck in a house with people I didn't know, in a place I'd never been to, with an ex that I wasn't even talking to.

No friends, no family, nothing.

The one good thing out of all of it was that, on the island, they have free community gyms, and luckily one was a short walk away from where I was staying.

I trekked through the snow most days to escape into the weights room.

I would spend hours there.

My first complete solo flight happened at 21 years old.

Three airports, two planes, and one long, red-eyed trip back to Heathrow.

I literally collapsed into my mum's arms as soon as I spotted her at the arrivals gate.

There were a lot of tears shed that day and a lot of chocolate eaten.

I struggled to get over the breakup, especially as he

continued to message me daily, saying how I was still his best friend and that he still loved and cared about me, but we couldn't be together anymore.

It was torture.

He persisted in making my life hell. Even after we had both returned to the UK, he landed a week after me.

We still had five months left on our tenancy agreement on the house, and even though I obviously wouldn't be living there anymore, he requested that I pay him at least £100 per month towards the bills.

'Are you on fucking crack, mate?' That was my original thought.

Due to the fact I didn't fly home from Canada on the original booked date, and I didn't have a spare £2000 to get myself home early, he had paid for my ticket, and so he bloody should have.

However, He decided to try and take me to court, as apparently, I was refusing to pay him the money back. He lent it to me, didn't give it to me, apparently.

Yet he never even mentioned this previously, and it would never have even crossed my mind, to be honest.

He broke my heart and left me stranded in a foreign country. The least he could do was pay to get me home to my friends and family.

Arsehole.

In some ways, him being the C-word made the break up a little easier, as I hated him.

The case was chucked straight out of the courtroom. He didn't have a leg to stand on.

Dickhead.

He also lost his job because of how he had treated me, not that he would have dared step back in that place after.

He was hated there.

I never saw him again, but I believe he is now happily married with children.

Good for him.

Dean was my absolute rock throughout the whole shitstorm, and I am so grateful to still have him in my life.

I had so many friends messaging me. I don't know what I would have done if I didn't have such an amazing support system back then.

I originally joined the Military to pre-occupy myself. I needed something to completely take my focus, as I was struggling to deal with the breakup.

Fuck, he was everything to me.

I had never considering joining the Military before, ever.

I passed all the tests with flying colours, and then I made a choice to become a firefighter.

That was one job role that stood out to me, especially when the lady in the AFCO informed me that there were currently only ten serving female firefighters in the RAF.

I wanted to be the 11th.

It was the challenge I needed.

If the guys could pass all the basic and firefighter training sessions, then so could I.

Game on.

It was a cold February morning in 2014 when I attested the oath of allegiance.

Or attestation, as it is called.

It took over a year to complete the application process, and the medical was the weirdest experience of my life.

I had to strip down to my knickers and walk around the doctor's room imitating a duck.

Luckily, I wore my granny pants, but I was still slightly concerned.

I would have been more concerned if he had asked me to 'Quack' at the same time.

I, Amy Elizabeth Coutin,
do swear that I will be faithful and bear true allegiance to Her
Majesty Queen Elizabeth II, her heirs and successors and that
I will, as in duty bound, honestly and faithfully defend her
Majesty.

Ten weeks of basic training, followed by 17 weeks of firefighter training, lay ahead of me.

The cliché image of a bunch of recruits arriving at RAF Halton. To begin basic training with massively oversized bags and ironing boards under their arms was very much the reality.

We all looked like pack horses, unfit, struggling pack horses, and it felt like the first day of school all over again.

Whether you are male or female, 18 or 30, big and hench, or small and puny, this is a very nervous time for everyone.

I was shitting myself.

I was glad when I spotted a couple of other girls, hidden amongst all the blokes, looking just as anxious as me.

We made our way to a block, as instructed by some

helpful SATTs (Servicemen/women Awaiting Trade Training), and scanned a list of names on the door to see what room we were to be in for the next ten weeks.

All the females were on the bottom floor, all of us in one room, to be fair, there were only ten of us, and all of the guys were on the top two floors.

We just dumped our bags on our thin, plastic-covered beds, yes, plastic-covered, and headed to the briefing room for our initial 'welcome brief'.

We were told that we were 'Campion' intake, and then we went around the room and did the usual stand-up, say your name, why you joined the RAF, and an interesting fact about yourself.

'Hi, I'm Amy, I'm 24, I'm a keen gym bunny, and I joined because I like a man in uniform, and my ex was an utter wanker'.

A quick ice breaker and an easy way to get to know a bit about the group.

I always get nervous standing up and talking in front of a large crowd, but for some reason, that day, I was absolutely fine, despite the 30 plus eyes on me.

After all the small talk, we were given a list of duties to complete that evening before bed.

All I wanted to do was sleep.

I mean, the bed just seemed so, so appealing.

The list mainly consisted of labelling things – you had to label everything, I mean everything, even your bloody socks.

What a faff that was.

We also had to complete several forms ready for the next day.

And so, it all truly began.

Day one, and I can honestly say, out of the whole ten weeks, the first day was one of the worst for me.

It's the day where we got our initial kitting at clothing stores.

There's nothing fun, at all, about getting changed as quickly as you can in a tiny little curtained cubicle, where first you have to find the correct piece of clothing, amongst the absolute mountain of it that is in this box cubicle with you, unpack it, take bits of cardboard and clips off, get it on, and dress correctly in it, then parade outside in a perfect line, perfectly dressed.

All the above while getting yelled at to 'hurry the fuck up'.

My stress levels were out of the roof, and I was sweating my tits off.

Once we had all been fitted and kitted, we had the next struggle to put all the clothing we had just received in a bag and then carry it back to the block.

I hated my life.

The nightmare just progressed from here.

All that kit had to be labelled and ironed.

And when I say ironed, I don't just mean running the iron over the clothing as you would at home, oh no, we had a lesson on how to iron pleats and perfectly crisp creases in the sleeves and trouser legs.

If we made the slight error of a 'tramline', we had to start again. In fact, if we made any slight error at all, we had to start again, as the piece of clothing would be screwed up by the Corporal or Sergeant inspecting them and chucked on the floor.

Meanwhile, you just stand there, biting your tongue,

smiling sweetly, and nodding in agreement.

The first few nights, I and the girls were up until at least 2 am trying to get our ironing skills on point.
I have never been hot on ironing, and now, I don't even own an iron, let alone use the thing.
That's what a washing line is for, just hang everything upside down and ta-da, no creases.
Oh, and if you were wondering what we were wearing in the first part of training, green overalls, lovely, unfitted, over washed, well worn, green overalls.
The least flattering things on the entire planet.
They made my beautiful bum completely non-existent. I just looked like a green piece of cardboard with a head.

Mealtimes were stressful. It was always a frantic rush. Everyone at Halton had limited time to eat. Sometimes we would be stood in a queue for over 20 minutes, which meant around ten minutes to sloosh some grub on a plate and shovel it in our mouths as quickly as possible, then rush to our next tasking.
I hated it.
We were like prey at a watering hole, trying to replenish ourselves before getting eaten by a lion or crocodile.
Well, that's what it felt like anyway.
I'm a food lover, and I like to enjoy my food and savour every bite, not force it down and then struggle with indigestion for hours to follow.

The remainder of the first few days were filled with medicals, briefs, admin and fuelled on very little sleep. You end up with arms like pincushions from all the vaccinations and jabs.

I couldn't even tell you what jabs they were.

We then had a foot drill (marching) added into the equation.

This meant hours and days on end, outside on the drill yard, practicing our 'left, right, lefts' in all weathers.

It was hilarious, to begin with, but got tedious quickly.

The laughing didn't last long at all, especially when it was pissing down with rain and cold.

There was a lot to take on board during the drilling phase, it really isn't a case of just 'marching', and I struggled not to get frustrated, but muscle memory soon came into effect, and things suddenly seemed to get easier.

Thank the Lord.

However, we were constantly reminded that none of it was a game.

A few people that were slightly lost causes by the drill didn't make it through to the next part of training.

Knowing your left and rights is sort of essential.

The evenings were rarely 'down time', with constant inspections and upcoming exams. We were all always busy cleaning, studying, or ironing.

I got on well with everyone on my intake.

I have always got on better with blokes than girls, so even though I did like all the females, I tended to hang out with the lads when I could.

Easier to talk to, less judgemental, and definitely more fun to be with.

You need a certain type of humour to be in the Military. Not everyone had that.

That made them the outcasts.

I was one of the cool kids.

A few of us met in the briefing room at the end of the evenings to polish our shoes and have a rant about the day.

I became close to one certain individual. We spent quite a bit of time together, had some fun, etc. I mean, he was a good laugh and quite a fit guy, but as soon as I found out he had false teeth, I was done.

I'm very vain.

With both myself and the person I'm with.

Looks always meant a lot to me, and well, they still do.

The image of him taking his teeth out was enough for me.

GST/GSK (General Service Training/Knowledge) makes up a big part of the first couple of weeks of basic training.

There was honestly so much to take in.

Constantly learning more and more about airpower, flight safety, regulations, health and safety, and all the other shite on top of it.

Then there's day 21, which is a well-known day in RAF basic training.

Day 21 is the day of the first big formal inspection.

An inspection that you pass or fail makes you stay in training or leave to go home.

There was a 'demo' bed space set up for us to imitate in our areas.

We had already been pre-warned by other recruits that loose threads on clothing and dust on furniture were major things to look out for.

Our beds, Military lockers, civvy lockers, and bedside tables had to be set out in a certain way with certain clothing items and wash kit items laid out in a precise way.

I still have no idea why our toothbrushes and toothpaste had to be involved in the inspections.

Maybe to make sure we had been brushing!?

We did have half a day of learning how to brush our teeth properly...

Don't ask.

On the day of inspection, I stood to attention at the end of my bed, which I'd taken three days to perfect, I even slept on the floor, so I didn't ruin my perfect hospital corners.

I do not miss them bad boys.

I was sweating by the time the sergeant made it to me. I remember looking dead straight ahead and trying not to move or breathe. I'd already seen one girl's bed flipped over as it wasn't up to standard. I was shitting myself and think I would have cried if I didn't pass.

Luckily, all the hard work and long nights paid off. I passed and finally breathed back out.

The formal inspection marks the end of the coverall phase.

I finally got to say goodbye to the horrible green denim overalls and could start to dress, primarily, in PCS (greens).

I loved wearing my greens. Not only were they super comfy, but not going to lie, I looked hot in them, as did the guys.

The next training phase I entered was IFPT (Initial

Force Protection Training) with the scary RAF regiment.

A brutal, physical, but enjoyable part of the course.

However, we had a whole week of AT (Adventurous Training) to look forward to first.

Probably one of my favourite times in the whole of the training phases. Half of my intake went to Fairbourne, and half went to Crickhowell.

I went to Crickhowell.

As soon as I arrived, the first thing I noticed was the beds, a proper mattress.

Heaven.

You don't even realise how much this means until you have slept on what feels like solid wood covered in cling film for weeks on end.

There was only me and two others in my room.

After sharing with eight others back at camp, that was bliss.

The guys had been sharing with double that, so they must have felt in absolute luxury having shared rooms of six while away.

Over the week of AT, we did many team-building challenges, which meant enhancing our followership and leadership skills.

The activities we did included kayaking, indoor climbing, hiking, camping, and navigation exercises, along with a bit of bushcraft.

I was in my element; I love being outdoors, and I love doing anything active.

One of the best memories was the navigation and camping. I was the only girl on my team at this point, and after a day of taking it in turns to navigate over hills and valleys in strong winds and rain, our newly learnt skills of building a campfire, and a camp, were set to the test.

It was a great evening.

We spent it roasting marshmallows over the fire, eating dinner out of rat packs, and all sat in a circle, laughing, with head torches stuck to our heads while wearing our matching red and blue waterproofs.

I have photos of this evening, and it really is one of my treasured memories.

Sam and Scott, everyone is known by their surnames in the Military, but I won't use them here, were two of the lads I got on well with from the start, and who to this day, I still love like my brothers, especially Sam who I shared many RAF adventures with, and he is mentioned throughout the next few chapters.

The week flew by, and it was a much-needed 'break'. However, we knew it was just the calm before the storm.

Back at Halton, the hard work began.

IFPT started.

I cried a lot of girly tears in this part of the training.

I think a fair few recruits did, actually.

Guys and girls.

Regiments are tough bastards.

They even look terrifying, well, some of them anyway, and so when they get right up in your face and yell at you while showering you in spit, shit, it is scary and very unpleasant.

The training didn't start off too painfully, three days of first aid training, all the basics, plus learning things like how to apply a tourniquet.

There was a written and a practical exam to pass.

CBRN (Chemical, Biological, Radioactive, and

Nuclear) training was next in our schedule, and it's arguably one of the most gruelling parts of the course. Suited and booted in a confining CBRN suit learning how to manoeuvre my way around a respirator (gas mask in layman's terms, but never call it a gas mask in front of the Regiment) was just delightful.

Once again, there were many theory lessons in between all the practical, with a wide range of information to note down.
It became more and more of a challenge to stay awake as they weren't the most engaging topics.
A couple of lads were pretty much passed out at their desks, so it wasn't long before they had pens and pencils thrown at them from an instructor, followed by 'Wake up, you bastards'.
The main aspect of CBRN, and possibly one of the most defining and memorable moments of Halton, is 'initial exposure,' AKA getting dragged into a building filled with CS gas, taking your life-saving respirator off, and dying for as long as is deemed necessary.
Initial exposure is supposed to make you trust your equipment.
You can walk into that building all suited up with your respirator on and feel nothing, but you know it's working because when you take it off, you feel everything.

There were about ten of us inside the chamber at one time, and one by one, standing in front of the Corporal, we were to shout out our name, rank, and number. There was one rule – no laughing. If you laughed at someone, you'd be staying in there longer.
I took off my respirator and instantly couldn't breathe

or open my eyes.

Everything was burning.

It was a vile experience, which seemed to get worse once you were back outside in the fresh air. Everything stung, your face, eyes, skin, throat, lips, everything. Honestly, everyone who came out of the room looks like a possessed zombie.

It was hilarious. To watch, not to experience.

You had no dignity at all by the end of it. You're just a walking, barely talking, dribbling, snotty mess.

Your nose would stream, as would your eyes, and you had to fight to urge not to chuck up.

Not the most attractive of looks.

If I were to write about it on TripAdvisor, I would give it a solid 1/10. I would not recommend it unless you want to experience death, a slow, painful death.

Safe to say, I was glad when that phase of the course was over.

However, I was unexpectedly super shit in the next chapter of training.

Weapon/Rifle drill.

Before we got to do any real shooting, we had to learn all about the weapon.

We quickly learnt never to call it a gun. It was always a weapon or rifle.

We had to learn all the individual components, how they worked, how to clean them, how to disassemble them and put them back together.

We spent a long time learning all this and had to pass a weapons handling test before learning how to use it.

I was fine with this aspect of it. It was the shooting and aiming I had a problem with.

Before we hit the live ranges, we had to learn all the shooting positions and practice firing in a range simulator, which is a case of shooting at targets on a screen.

I struggled to get my breathing right, and my aim was embarrassing. I always thought I'd be a good shot, be oh no, I was shooting like I was blind.

I even had to have extra tuition. When you have the RAF regiment guys laughing in your face about how shit you are, it makes it ten times harder to relax, and I honestly felt like jacking it all in right there and then.

I didn't, obviously.

I did get better, and I did somehow manage to pass.

Fuck knows how.

The live range was fun, to be honest, but obviously, there was no room for errors.

Safety was a big thing, and the last thing you'd want was an error during the drill or a negligent discharge (ND).

We were responsible for 'bombing up' (putting rounds in) our magazines, doing all the correct drills, firing accurately, unloading, and doing the relevant safety drills at the end.

It was all about being precise, not rushing anything, and always listening to what we were told.

I was grateful it was over and even more grateful I was still there.

'Exercise Blue Warrior' now stood ahead of us, and this was where we had to apply everything we had learnt up till now.

We loaded all of our jam-packed bags onto a Military truck and headed to the armoury, where we all got issued a weapon.

This rifle went EVERYWHERE with me.

I toileted with it, slept with it, and ate with it. I did everything with it.

If any of us were seen with our weapon more than an arm's length away at any one point during the exercise, they got a beasting right there and then.

Blue Warrior is where most of the re-flights come from at Halton.

It was the test of all tests.

We had to pass.

After a short coach journey, we arrived at the exercise location, our home for the next few days, which was a filthy, empty hangar, in the middle of fields and woodland, with no doors, which seemed to somehow be colder than it was outside.

It was a very full-on few days, filled with super early mornings and long nights on patrol.

Meals were various rat packs which we had to cook in small metal, mess tins on our little Hexi stoves, and they were a bastard to clean.

The days were spent creeping and crawling through the trees and undergrowth with our rifles, hiding behind bushes, working as a team to deal with various tasks and challenges, and generally applying all the knowledge we had learnt in the IFPT phase.

On, I think, the third day came the 'Square of death' this was something we had all heard rumours about.

It was a very physically demanding exercise, and we all became unimaginably broken, sore, wet, and muddy.

It rained the whole time, involved a lot of commando crawling and running, and drove us all to physical exhaustion.

The final day, despite being knackered, was good fun, the final firefight, which involved an all-out war to get rid of the last of the rounds we all had.

It was utter chaos and a really good way to end the exercise.

However, the brutal body torture hadn't ended yet. We had to 'tab' to the coach, with all our kit. This was hell for me, my legs burned, and every inch of my body ached from the day's activities. I was one of the few at the back; I struggled. My body wanted to give up.

I cried, but no sympathy came my way. I was yelled at and shouted at, which never makes things easier, but eventually, I made it back.

I felt dead.

I think that is exactly what dying feels like.

When we arrived at Halton, there was no rest period, it was time to clean our rifles, and they were bloody filthy.

It went eerily quiet. Everyone was just kneeling, stripping their weapons, and cleaning as best they could.

Following this, we had a post-CPT inspection to get ready for. This meant a manic weekend of washing, ironing, and even more washing.

The good news was that that inspection marked the end of the greens phase.

From here on, we were only wearing our smart blue shirts and trousers, no more casual, comfy PCS.

This is where we began our graduation preparation.

We were all pretty good at drill by now, so we did find it quite amusing watching new courses attempt to march in time.

However, things got a bit more complicated when we had to include a rifle and learn new drill moves using it while marching.

By the end of the week, my arms were covered in bruises from whacking the rifle against my biceps.

It took a while to get into the groove of marching with a rifle, more so for certain individuals.

'Change arms' was one of the moves I found most challenging. It is essentially swapping the rifle into your other arm in a quick but smooth manner while trying not to stab yourself in the hand with the bayonet.

Such fun.

Long days and nights were spent on the parade square practicing all the drills. A few others and I even borrowed some wooden rifles so we could practice the drills in our downtime.

Thinking back to that, all that comes to mind is that we must have looked like utter dickheads.

Nobody wanted to fail this late into training, especially when graduation was now only a couple of weeks away, so we were doing everything we could, no matter how embarrassing or stupid.

One last major hurdle stood between us all and the 'finish line'.

One last pass or fail, and an area where many people do fail.

The time had come for the big, scary final inspection.

Day 63.

The amount of prep needed for the final inspection is monumental.

In addition to what we already had presented in our Military lockers, we needed at least another shirt, maybe two, some more trousers, shoes, and everything set out in the exact way we'd been shown.

Our bed spaces had to be precise and spotless.

I remember the night before the final inspection really well because about half of our courses were up until about 3 am making the final touches.

You are supposed to sleep in your bed every single night, and anyone caught will be disciplined.

Almost everyone slept on the floor that night.

I made my bed immaculately at 2 am, and I was not going to touch it again, so I opted for a few uncomfortable hours on the floor also, as I did in the previous big inspections.

As well as the bed, some of us needed to re-label pretty much all of the kit (with green sniper tape and stencils, which took ages and was very tedious), dust relentlessly, cleans the mirrors to perfection, and hoover pretty much everything.

I would go as far as saying that I would lick the floors. It was that bloody spotless.

The morning soon came, and I recall getting up extra early, sleeping for about two hours to make sure I was as clean and presentable as my bed space and lockers.

We had to be dressed in our full number one uniform, which meant being the most uncomfortable you could be.

The top button on the shirt was choking me, and the

braces were digging into my shoulders.

Waiting at the end of the bed for the door to open was one of the most nerve-racking parts of training.

We were stood by our beds for almost two hours, waiting for the inspection to take place.

Sweaty palms don't even cut it.

Thankfully I passed and breathed a massive sigh of relief, and now I could solely focus on perfecting my arms drill and graduation.

The last week was exclusively arms practice and the dress rehearsal.

The rehearsal gets watched by some senior officers and the Station Commander.

I think the decision comes down to him or someone of equal importance whether the standard of the dress rehearsal is good enough for you to graduate the following day.

I can vaguely remember a course having to delay their graduation because they made too many mistakes on the rehearsal. Hence, it was something we had to nail as an intake.

Rehearsing with the real marching band is a lot different from marching along to a CD being played. So, it's something that, again, takes a while to get used to, plus, it was bloody loud.

Graduation day arrived.

The sun was shining high in the cloudless, blue sky, and everyone was grinning from ear to ear. We had made it.

An emotional but brilliant day all around.

Our family and friends all got to come and watch, we

couldn't actually speak to them until after our big parade, but it was lovely to know they were watched, and so nice to just see them all again.

Graduation is such a proud moment. When you watch yourselves back on camera and see how smart you look, how perfectly we were all marching in time, and how we were carrying out all the drills flawlessly, with the red arrows flying overhead, you can't help but smile and also feel slightly overwhelmed.

I can't explain how incredible it all was and what a relief it was that the hard work had paid off immensely.

I had my Mum, Dad, Gran, and Nan there.

A day I will always remember, even more so now that my lovely Nan isn't around.

We got to have drinks, which wasn't the best idea, I was half pissed and couldn't undo the buttons on my shirt, so I just ripped my way out of it like the hulk.

Oops.

Thank God I had lots of spares.

Halton really was just a game.

That's all it ever was and all it ever will be.

You learn a hell of a lot and grow so much as a person, but the real test is just being able to follow orders and have the right 'can-do' attitude.

If you can do that, you can get through it with no problem whatsoever.

Not going to lie, I hated most of it at the time, but looking back now, it wasn't so bad.

I met some great people, made some of the most memorable memories, and became an even tougher bitch.

My life in the Military had begun. I was no longer a 'Miss' but now known as 'LAC' Coutin (Leading aircraftsman).

4 BOOTS, BUNKERS, BALL SACKS, AND BOOZE

"Remember why you started, don't give up, find a way."

With Halton and basic training finally over, things were about to get even tougher.
And hotter.
And much sweatier.
Who wants a quiet life anyway, eh?
Next in my RAF journey, I moved down to sunny Kent to complete my 17 weeks of firefighter training at RAF Manston.

'Crash fire rescue is one of the most aggressive firefighting disciplines requiring courage and professionalism. RAF Firefighters form a part of the Force Protection recuperation element for Defence when operating in the UK and overseas. You will receive exceptional training to ensure you are adequately prepared to respond and resolve incidents involving aircraft, buildings, vehicles, hazardous substances, and incidents caused by hostile activities.'

There was a bar, 'Blues and Twos', on-site, and the beach was only a short drive down the road, and it was the middle of summer, absolutely winning, or so I thought.

I soon discovered I was not winning at all, wearing a full fire kit, with boots that weighed a ton, while running around in boiling sunshine, dragging 70kg hoses into fires, really is not too pleasant.

I was sweating from places that I didn't even know existed while being surrounded by attractive blokes. Guys, if you are reading this, that comment only applied to a handful of you, I couldn't feel less sexy.

We were all showering at least twice a day.

However, if you want to lose weight, I highly recommend doing a firefighter training course.

The first week at Manston was pretty standard, kit fittings for our bunkers, jackets and boots, a shit load of admin, and getting to find our way around the place.

It was nice as a good chunk of my intake was also on my Halton course, so I knew the majority, Sam and Scott were there too.

There were only two other females on my fire training. The rest were all blokes, which suited me just fine.

Plus, I was the only straight one out of the three of us. Wink, wink, nudge, nudge.

We were treated more like adults at Manston, and it was slightly more relaxed. Plus, our instructors were absolute legends. We could have a laugh with them but at the same time respect them and work hard when required.

There was a hell of a lot to learn, and once again, most of our downtime was filled with revision and studying.

We did let our hair down, maybe a bit too much, at the weekends, days playing volleyball at the beach, nights spent drinking down 'The Dolphin' in Margate, and early mornings spent 'after partying' in the block.

The drinking and parties were nothing compared with what I got up to once stationed at my first base... but that's later in the story.

Weeks one through to four was the least exciting of the course, for me anyway, fire extinguisher maintenance and fire service drills.

This meant learning which first aid fire appliance/fire extinguisher (FAFA) extinguishes what type of fire and how to service them and check them, blah, blah, blah.

This meant paperwork.

Yawn, I know, but still extremely important and an essential part of being in the fire service.

Unfortunately.

I spent a fair bit of time in the station gym, and if we ever finished early or had a night off from studying, I'd be in the gym lifting the iron.

I was losing weight and muscle from the sheer amount of cardio. We had to 'tab' everywhere, and when you are in a full fire kit 90% of the time, you quickly lose body fat without even trying.

I wanted my little girly guns back and my arse.

Even though I was surrounded by men 24/7, none of them were really boyfriend material, not that I was even looking for anything serious, but I had been single since the ginge, and was only getting older, so I was always keeping my eye out in some respect.

I didn't want to grow ancient, alone, being surrounded by cats.

There were drunken fumbles with a few of the guys, but that was all, and probably for the best anyway. Militant personnel aren't exactly known to be the most faithful of people on the planet.

Very stereotypical, but true, I can vouch for that. I've lived, worked, and slept, with enough of them over the years to know this.

They all have tinder accounts, regardless of their relationship status.

I did begin to struggle with some of the written aspects of the course, and I have always found it difficult to retain information, especially when trying to take in so much of it on so many varied topics.

I needed to know everything about hazardous substances, fire safety, buildings, and things like how to figure out dimensions and depths, volumes, how much water would be needed, all Math like equations, and I hated Maths.

I wrote notes on every subject and stuck bright pink and yellow post-it notes all around my tiny bed space in the hope of digesting the information.

It didn't work, and I was failing the exams.

I'm not, and wasn't, stupid. In fact, I like to think I am pretty switched on. I did well in English and Maths in both school and college, so why, as I got older, was I finding it so hard?

Was dementia kicking in super, super early?

Fuck knows.

I was smashing all the practical aspects. I am very much a visual, hands-on learner, which was proven but put me in a classroom in exam conditions, and I go blank.

After getting extremely upset, frustrated, and angry at the whole situation, one of our amazing instructors took the time to provide me with some extra tuition, I felt like such a twat, being one of those 'special' students, but at the end of the day, if I didn't have it, I would have failed the course and wouldn't have done half the things that I have done, and achieved, now.
Sometimes asking for help, or accepting help, is the bravest move you can make.
It doesn't make you weak. It reveals strength, even when you don't feel strong, and trust me, in those days and hours, I felt weaker than a cup of tea that my sister makes.
Which means hot milk.

The breathing apparatus (BA) phrase of the training was bloody brutal, but in a strange way, quite fun.
The sets were heavy to carry, and if you are short, like me, the sets take up your whole body.
Initially, it took a while to get used to performing all the 'before use' safety checks, but after plenty of practice, it became second nature, which was good as in training, and when in the job, you carry out these checks all the bloody time.
We soon moved on to road traffic incident techniques (RTIs or RTCs). This meant smashing windows, removing car roofs, cutting out full windscreens, and slashing seatbelts.

Any anger could be taken out here. It was highly satisfying to safely rescue the 'casualties', which were blow-up sex dolls.

Again, as with everything in training, it required a fair bit of practice to learn the correct techniques and memorise what tool was used for what.

There were a whole two lockers full of RTC equipment on the fire appliance (fire engine, but we weren't allowed to call it that).

We had to learn each different crash scenario.

Car on roof, car on the side, car on fire, conscious casualty, unconscious casualty, location of the crash, the list goes on.

You never realise how in-depth it all is and how important it is to quickly think on your feet when in the emergency services.

Confidence came with experience.

My confidence was low at the start of every new phrase we endured.

I hated being watched while doing something new. My body just flooded with anxiety at the thought of doing it wrong or being laughed at, which really was pathetic as we were all in the same boat and all were learning these things for the very first time.

Despite always feeling nervous, I never had any issues passing any part of the practical exams.

They were tough and took every ounce of your mental and physical energy, but as long as you listened to every detail of the task and performed safely, you were fine.

At least, practically, I was bossing it all.

Fuck the written crap.

Aircraft construction, and crash rescue and operations, was the pinnacle of training.

We were all there training to be crash rescue (as in aircraft crash) and domestic firefighters.

We had completed the domestic part, so next was the crash.

This was certainly the most intense part of the course. I was learning how to shut down engines on massive aircraft in emergencies, evacuate the passengers, make the aircraft safe, and obviously, how to extinguish a fire on an aircraft.

This was big. This is what the training was all about. This is what we would be doing in the Real World at our RAF base stations... or so we thought.

It was interesting to learn how all the buttons and handles in a cockpit worked. It was even more interesting deploying a vehicle and running around with massive foam hoses to extinguish big arse engine fires.

Instant adrenaline rush.

'Hot cans' was another delightful task we had to take part in. It was a case of being sat inside a compact metal barrel while it was on fire.

Heat acclimation.

Lovely.

I remember feeling like I was dying from the heat, but at the same time, watching the flames dance above my head was mesmerising and quite therapeutic.

I wouldn't recommend staying in them for a long period.

As the weeks went on, we continued to learn more and more and take part in constant live practice fires

and scenarios, which ended up with assessments.
Yay.

One of the main passes or fail aspects was a house fire rescue mission, which had a partial building collapse. There were three casualties within the two-story building, one adult and two children.

Working within our BA pairs, we had to safely extinguish the fire and rescue the casualties.

The pressure was on, and there was no room for error. Communication was key, as was working perfectly as a team.

I was BA number one, which meant I was 'the leader', after carrying outdoor checks to make sure we weren't at risk of backdraft, I slowly made my way into the smoke-filled hallway, laying a guideline as we went, and doing the 'BA shuffle' that we had learnt (checking all around you with your hands and feet, which looks like you are performing some weird '80s dance move).

The whole time I could feel my little heart pounding in my chest and feel the beads of sweat running down my back and forehead.

I could barely see in front of me.

Thankfully, we located the casualties and safely extracted them one by one, carrying out the casualty handling techniques we had practiced over the previous weeks.

The dummies replicated the weight of real people, so the adult casualty was bloody heavy, around 80kg, carrying him, a hose, a guideline, and being weighed down with your BA set isn't the easiest of tasks, but we did it, and both passed with flying colours.
Phew.

Being strong, and I'm not going to say 'strong for a

female', because I'm just strong in general, stronger than some blokes, but it is essential.

One of the other girls physically struggled with the weight of some equipment and the casualties.

Living and breathing the gym definitely paid off in some parts of the course.

Our 17 weeks of running around like headless chickens soon ended, and we were, once again, preparing for another graduation.

This one was very different from Halton. We put on a show for everyone to watch, including friends and family who were allowed to come and see everything we had learnt.

We practiced the 'routine' over and over. There were two aircraft on fire and an oil spill in flames.

We each had different roles to carry out. Some were firefighting, some were rescuing casualties, some were assisting others, and I was a runner, joys of joys.

I had the task of being everyone's bitch.

So, getting the ladders off the truck, getting different hose attachments, helping with firefighting, literally just running around like a lunatic.

I didn't even like running at all.

Once we had completed the 'show', we had all the formalities and award ceremonies to get through.

March, salute, get a certificate, pat on the back, carry on.

Everyone headed to the bar after getting changed and celebrated with all the guests that had come to see us.

It was a nice, pissed as fuck, evening.

My sister, Anna, and Mum and Dad had come to watch the graduation, I hadn't seen them in a while, so it was lovely.

They stayed in a nearby hotel, and I think I went back with them for dinner. I can't really remember, maybe I stayed there? Who knows, I was pretty drunk. Standard.

I just remember Anna hooked up with one of the fire lads.

That's my girl.

Fist bump.

I was then stationed at RAF Coningsby in Lincolnshire.

Home of the fast jets.

The incredible Tornadoes and Typhoons, and the Battle of Britain aircraft, including the Spitfire and Dakota, were based there.

That was to be my initial three-year posting, with a fair few of those months also spent up in beautiful RAF Lossiemouth, Scotland.

And the Falkland Islands.

I can safely say those years held the most fun I've ever had, mainly due to the company.

I worked with a great bunch of lads.

I have told them about this book and how they will feature in this chapter, one response I got was, 'Once upon a time, I joined the RAF, caused a lot of shit, then left'.

He sums it up pretty well.

Another said, 'Amy, some of us are still in, so make sure you keep the stories chilled, yeah, so much shit went down'.

I was on red watch, and I was the only female firefighter at Coningsby. In fact, I was the first female firefighter they had stationed there in years, apparently.

Go me!

I worked a variation of day shifts, night shifts, and 24-hour shifts.

You would be bored if I were just to tell you all about the 'work' we did, as there weren't exactly many fires, the majority of the call-outs we got were for people burning toast or birds, the flying kind, setting alarms off in the hangers.

I suppose we did have a few interesting shouts, a couple of 'mayday' calls for engine fires, and such.

We were primarily there to look after the aircraft.

If the jets were to get called out, we would be on the runway as a 'just in case', in 'state three' positions.

State one meant 'it's fucked, it's crashed, it's a goner'.

State two meant 'the aircraft's in shit, go help'.

State three meant 'nothing's happened yet, but it might, so sit on standby just in case'.

I learnt how to shut down the jets and also how to make the ejection seats safe and rescue the pilot.

There was a lot of training.

A hell of a lot of training tests, and all had to be passed to be promoted and move up in ranks.

I did pass and received my promotion to Senior Aircraftsman (SAC), which meant more pay and no longer the brew bitch on crew.

It also meant promotion pizza night.

Winning!

On night shifts and 24-hour shifts, I shared the bedroom with the lads. Waking up in the morning with five blokes in the room really isn't pleasing on the nostrils.

73

Sweaty ball sacks, farts, and B.O.

Delightful.

I rarely slept, no one did, as we were often woken to a mattress to the face, a duvet pulled off, flashing disco lights, or sometimes even a locker on top of you.

We took it in turns to pull pranks on each other.

One time, my shirt was put through the shredder, and I had to walk back to the block looking like I'd been mauled by a tiger.

I found it funny.

Some pranks didn't always play out too well, though.

I stupidly decided to pull a prank on one of our corporals.

I set up a fake tinder account and was messaging this black guy, and I gave him my corporal's number. Obviously, he thought it was mine and asked him to send dick pics.

At the time, my Corporal was away on a training course at Manston.

In the middle of that course, he was in fluxed with big black dicks all over his phone screen.

Unfortunately, he didn't find this too amusing, he found out it was me, and I got in shit.

I had to give presentations to all the fire crews on personal data breaches.

The guys all found it hilarious, though, and I won even more lad points.

So, who's the real champion here?

On another occasion, a lad off another crew, Neil, had been messaging me. I was on shift at the time, so all the guys saw the messages.

Prank time was ideal.

I texted Neil back and told him I was horny and

asked him to talk dirty to me as I was about to go and have a shower.

He instantly replied with some corny dirt followed with 'Take a pic of you in the shower', I told him I would if he sent me a dick pic.

Therefore, not only did the whole red watch see his little willy, but Neil got his shower pic.

All the lads in the shower together laughing, we were clothed, well undies were on anyway.

Poor Neil was mortified.

Luckily, he did see the comical side, and all was well at work the next day.

But anyway, onto the even more fun stuff.

Due to the stories I am about to tell you and the fact that some of the people in my stories are still in the services, all the names are fictional.

On my initial, crew there was me, Max, Grayson, James, Oliver, and Noah.

We were the dream team.

They all ripped me to pieces, to begin with, until they soon realised that I was actually cool and just 'one of the lads'.

You MUST be able to take banter in the Military, well in the RAF fire service for sure, especially being a female, or you will get bullied the shit out of.

Take shit and give shit.

That's just the way it is.

We went out on the piss a lot, and we would hit it hard and got in trouble or mischief almost every time.

Together, the six of us, we were bloody wild.

I had to keep up with the lads, which wasn't flipping easy, but I did it, well, tried.

Most times, it ended in me blackout drunk, but I tried.

They always looked out for me. They were like my brothers, well, all except Max and James, who I ended up in bed with on many drunken occasions.

Mainly, Max, it was almost always Max.

Both taken, by the way, I told you that you shouldn't trust Military blokes.

Honestly, the majority of the men I got with while in the RAF were married, or at least in a relationship. I didn't always know this at the time.

On one night out in Revolutions, Lincoln, I, and the lads got kicked out and barred.

Max and I couldn't wait to get back to camp that night as we had sex right there and then, against the bar, in a packed club.

I remember Oliver saying that he could see my black dress pulled up and my little pink knickers on the floor, then instantly twigged at what was going on.

Classy bird me.

Sorry, Mum, don't be mad. I'm classy now, I promise.

We continued in the alley outside before heading onto the next place to get even more smashed-off triple vodka red bulls.

On a completely separate occasion, there were bloody loads of them. We made a massive cocktail bucket as a pre-drink. I think it had over ten bottles of spirits in it.

Animals.

Before we went out, I used to head up to the all-male firefighter corridor on the top floor of my block for pre-drinks with the lads.

We polished the bucket off then went to town.

We should have called it quits after town, but oh no, back to the block for even more drinks.

That night a lot of shit went down.

A lot of shit.

The block was completely trashed. There were even tiles missing from the ceiling and explosions in the microwave.

Plus, it reeked of booze.

And vomit.

The block was only a couple of years old.

The next morning notices were put up around the halls asking for people to come forward with information.

We were in a ton of shit.

Well, actually, Max was.

He was the only one living in that corridor at the time, so the only firefighter that could be pinned down to being there.

All other trades instantly dobbed the firefighters in.

We weren't well liked as a trade.

Mainly as we were wreck heads and home wreckers, in more respect than one.

A few months after being at Coningsby, I got assigned to assist with the Royal International Air Tattoo (RIAT).

Jeez, what a week that was.

I think I'm still recovering now.

It was awesome, and I loved it.

I didn't know any of the guys, but they all knew me or had heard about me, so lots of fresh meat, and boy, some of that meat was hot.

We all shared a weird wooden cabin with separate bunk bedrooms.

'Club Echoes' was soon formed, we converted one of the rooms into our drinking area, and all met there every night to get utterly shitfaced.

'House every weekend' and 'Heads will roll' will forever remind me of RIAT.

It's good luck that we didn't get any call-outs. We were all hanging out of our arses in the daytime.

Every daytime.

To be fair, the days were spent sat on the side of the runway, in the sun, watching the air show. It was decent. People paid to watch it, and we were getting paid to watch it.

I wasn't big into planes, but the show was fascinating all the same, and nice to be doing something different with a new crowd.

I ended up liking one of the guys I met there, well, two of them, in fact, both firefighters, and they were best mates.

I initially started spending evenings with one of them, Paul, late nights of passion on tables under gazebos and cheeky fondling sessions in the bunks.

Then Evan came into the equation, one drunken night with him and how the feelings turned, I genuinely got on very well with him, drunk and sober, and even after leaving the RAF, I stayed in touch with him.

He did have the most amazing smile, and we shared a lot of passions.

I still stalk him on Instagram, actually.

A good friendship was also formed with another guy, Lindon.

It was just a close friendship, and nothing ever

happened between us.

I don't know why it didn't.

We spent one of the RIAT nights having a random late-night picnic in the car park while stargazing, it was such a laugh, and nice to get away from all the other drunken antics going on at the bar – Naked pullups, and trust me, that's not always something you want to see.

I remember how we were both properly belly laughing with tears streaming down our cheeks over ridiculous things.

One of the best feelings in the World.

I spoke to Lindon every day without fail for a good few years and still speak to him now on the odd occasion.

He is one of those people who could make me laugh regardless of the circumstances and what kind of mood I was in.

He has gorgeous arms too.

After returning to Coningsby, I soon got sent up to the Highlands in bonnie, Scotland, for a month, where I fell in love with the place and a guy.

I was based at RAF Lossiemouth, which is just a coastal path walk away from some of the most beautiful places I've ever been.

Hopeman and Burghead.

They quickly became two of my favourite places to go on days off.

I have been back a few times since then, on holiday.

I was once again on a crew with a load of new lads. Who, thankfully, I all got on well with.

I seemed to always get on well with everyone, a trait I

am very grateful for.

One of my corporals caught my eye quite soon on.

And vice versa.

Not my usual type, more dad bod than gym bod.

He started messaging me within just hours of arriving.

It wasn't until a few days later that I saw the ring on his finger.

Married, bloody typical.

But that stopped nothing.

I started meeting him out of work, and we were constantly speaking.

On days we worked together, we would meet up in the locker room, or control room, for a quick kiss, or he would assign me to go on FAFA checks around the station with him.

On a couple of occasions, we had more than a kiss in the back of the van.

I know it was bad, and all were going to end in tears, but I was falling for him.

He was a good-looking guy, fun to be around. He showered me in compliments and made me feel special.

He said and did all the right things.

I even went round to his house a few times.

That was tough, photos of him and his Mrs all around the place. How could he even be doing this to her?

Yes, I was just as wrong, but when we first started talking, I had no idea she even existed.

Then it was too late.

He was always honest with me about things.

I knew nothing could properly happen between us.

He had a child as well as a wife.

However, he told me he loved me, which made things so much harder.

I went out on the piss with the other lads on crew most weekends, and we used to do tourist things in the day – Loch Ness, Aviemore, Cairngorms, shopping, distilleries, then hit the pubs in the evenings.

Deep down, I was hurting because of the whole married guy situation, so I made sure I had as much fun as possible and tried to deter my mind.

On one occasion, my 'fun' went viral on the internet.

On Twitter, actually.

Me and one of the fire lads I was out with ended up in a pub doorway, erm, and the video was me with something in my mouth.

It wasn't a cigarette.

It was broad daylight.

On a busy Saturday afternoon.

Enough said there.

Mr love affair didn't like that I 'had cheated' at all.

I think he kind of forgot that he was undeniably the one doing all the cheating.

He genuinely didn't speak to me for like four days because of it.

When I wasn't working, drinking, or hanging out with the guys, I did a lot of hiking and exploring in Scotland, I absolutely loved it up there, and I still do.

Miles and miles of beautiful coastal paths, scenic, tranquil lakes, and impressive snow-capped mountains.

I have been back up for short breaks on many occasions, and I would happily live there, to be honest. It's one of my all-time favourite places.

Lake Morlich, in Aviemore, is one of the most

beautiful places I have ever been and one of my favourites.

Go there, or at least Google it.

The walk takes you through enchanted woodland, across pretty wooden bridges, even along a stretch of sandy beach, all the while the impressive Cairngorm mountains loom in the distance.

Apparently, there are occasional Osprey sightings at the lake, and I wasn't lucky enough to spot any there. Still, I did visit the nearby Osprey sanctuary to see the magnificent birds. They were awaiting their chicks to hatch at the time.

Another one of my most memorable Scottish hikes is when I first climbed Ben Macdui, with some of the lads, the second-highest 'Munro' (mountain) in Scotland and in Britain, and much wilder than Ben Nevis.

It is located in the Cairngorms national park amongst other numerous Munro's.

The sun was beaming down, pretty purple heather laced the small white track, and the sky was a deep cornflour blue.

It was cold, but still the perfect conditions.

The panoramic views were utterly stunning, and it didn't matter which direction I looked. There was a breath-taking scene to be gawped at.

The terrain was highly undulating, but the incline was gradual, making the long trek fairly bearable.

The higher up we got, the colder it became.

Our navigation skills, between us, were horrendous. You wouldn't have thought we had all passed basic training.

We got lost, somehow, and all stood huddled around

a compass like utter dickheads, arguing which way was the right way.

We guessed.

Luckily, we guessed right.

Before the final summit, I was knee-deep in snow, and that's not even an exaggeration.

It was bloody hard to walk through, you had to laugh, or you'd cry.

The summit track was completely hidden under the bright white blanket, and it became steep.

Really steep.

At one point, I was on my hands and knees, as were a couple of the guys.

Totally worth the damp clothes, though.

An overwhelming burst of joy hit me once I smacked my palm down on the gold summit marker.

Seventeen kilometres, and just over four hours later, we had hit the peak.

No words could describe the views that day, the skies were pure blue, and there wasn't a cloud in sight, making the furthest of places visible.

It was downright beautiful.

It completely absorbed you, and for a short period, all I could do was stop and stare and just breathe in the purity of it all.

I had climbed in once more since then, and I intend and doing it a third also.

Once my four-week posting was over. I returned to Lincolnshire, and I immediately put myself forward to go back up to Scotland.

None of the guys ever wanted to go up, but I loved it there for numerous reasons.

Within a few weeks, I was back in my custard yellow

car, embarking on the 12-hour drive up to Morayshire.

That 'visit' was all about exploring.

I discovered fairy tale castles, picturesque lakes, pretty little seaside towns, riverside walkways, and secret disused railway tracks in enchanted forests.

I could go into detail about every place I went, but I could easily write enough to fill a separate book.

If you have never been to the Highlands or Speyside, seriously, get it on your to-do list, you will not regret it at all!

Talking of Scotland, a fond relationship was created between myself and a Scottish Sergeant who started working at Coningsby, Gordie, I bloody loved him, and still do, he is a top bloke, we spent some time out of work together, as friends, and to this day we keep in touch.

He taught me that only gentlemen walk on the roadside of the path when with a lady.

He was always interested in what I had to say and genuinely liked my company, I could tell.

He is an old bugger, about ten years older than me, and did look out for me like a Father would, and he still does now, to be honest.

I guess he is the one that got away, really.

Love you, G.

5 FOUR MONTHS IN THE FALKLAND ISLANDS

"When you are grateful, fear disappears, and abundance appears."

Dressed in my sexy camo greens, sat in a tiny room at RAF Brize Norton, loaded up with two massive black ops bags, I awaited the 19-hour flight to the Falkland Islands.

I heard from many of the guys, who had been on tour there, that it was the most boring placement in the World, but a few others told me they relished in the wild nature of the seals and penguins over a war-torn tour in another land.

I ended up loving my deployment.

Friends and family had told me to enjoy my time in Scotland or how jealous they were I was going to a tropical paradise, so I'm not exactly going on a whim by saying a fair few people don't know where this is near-Arctic Archipelago sits.

If you don't know where the Falklands are, the Islands are located off the Southeast coast of South

America, just above Antarctica.
Definitely not a Caribbean-like island.

Just before landing, a safety video popped up on the TV screens above us, and an info-film that could well have been made in the '90s came on advising us about biosecurity, the wildlife country code, and not to go for a jog on the airport runway.
I started to wonder at this point just how far we had travelled, was it closer to 19 hours or 19 years.
Visiting the Falkland Islands was like stepping back in time. It is one of the strangest places I had ever been, yet one of the richest in wildlife and weather.

The first thing I noticed was the sideways trees.
It gets so windy on the Islands that the few trees they have are blown sideways and seem to stay that way.
There are no native trees that survive on the remote land. The ones there were planted in 1983, one year after the Falklands war ended.
The rest of the terrain was covered in rocks, mountains, and green tufts of grass, with an odd plant here and there.
It seemed completely barren.
My initial Falkland diary entry began with:
'What the hell is this place? Where are the houses? Where are the people? Where is anything?'

I was met by the fire lad I was replacing. He helped with my luggage and showed me to my room.
There was a firefighter corridor of rooms, three men per room, however as I was the only female firefighter, yet again, I had to be upstairs with a random bird who worked in military transport (MT).

The dorm-style room was more basic than Halton.
The showers were vile.
The toilets weren't any better, and they were on the ground floor.
The curtains were hanging off the rails, and I had one locker to keep four months' worth of shit in.
Home sweet home.

I was on the crash fire crew rather than domestic, which I was happy about as that's what I knew from Coningsby.
The shift pattern was 24 hours on, 24 hours off.
The guys were all alright. It was a much bigger crew than I was used to, so I was nervous at first, as again, I knew nobody, and some lads were always funny about having a girl join the team.
I had to share a bedroom, and showers and toilets with the blokes.
The toilets and showers were in the same room.
I will never forget when I was enjoying my nice hot shower after a group 'Insanity' session, and Sam decided he needed to take a massive dump.
Splendid.

My first day off, which was day three of my tour, was epic.
A few of us planned a trip to 'Whale Point', named due to whale bones found all along the beach.
We had to follow a very rugged off-road trail in beat-up land rovers to get there, which was fun in itself.
We were bouncing all over the place, and for once, I was glad of only having small lemons and not massive melons.
It's a completely surreal experience being surrounded

by elephant seals, sea lions, albatrosses, and a million different penguins, all in their natural environment.

Some elephant seals were around four metres in length and must have weighed at least four thousand kilograms.

Further along the white sanded beach, we saw the shipwreck of St Mary, one of the many casualties of the challenges of rounding Cape Horn in the late 1800s.

Many photographs were taken this day

Days and nights on shift were very monotonous.

We would carry out various firefighter training along with all the usual daily jobs and tasks. We would get hot and sweaty in the bays while following along to Shaun T and his 'Insanity' workouts. We would watch TV, eat, and sleep.

Unless we got a call out, of course.

Which didn't happen too frequently.

The most night-time activity we got was the lowering, and raising, of the rotary hydraulic arrestor gear (RHAG), which is designed to stop fast jet aircraft in the event of an emergency landing, or aborted take-off, the pilot would lower a hook which would 'take the RHAG'.

It is a massive steel wire cable with periodically positioned rubber wheels which all had to be moved manually to lower and raise it.

The base at Mount Pleasant is one of a kind. Everything is connected by one never-ending corridor, the 'Death Star Corridor', and is, in fact, the World's longest corridor.

Over eight hundred metres long, and I had to walk that bastard daily.

It links the barracks, the messes, the gym, the library, the cinema, the bar, the welfare areas, and the shops.

I mean, facility-wise, the camp is amazing.

The gym and pool were insane, and I spent a lot of my free time there, mainly training with Sam. We both got on so well. I was his mother figure while we were away. He was like a lost puppy when he wasn't with me.

I knew Sam from Halton and Coningsby, and I was really glad when he joined me on the island a week after my arrival.

Nights in the bar were messy.

Very messy.

I had to be careful as I was one of the only females on the camp, thousands and thousands of RAF, Army, Navy, and Paratrooper blokes, but in numbers, there were easily a few hundred men to every female.

As soon as I walked into that bar, every time I stepped in that door, all eyes were on me.

It didn't matter if I was dressed up or just in jeans and a t-shirt. I could have been wearing a bin bag. It wouldn't have mattered.

Like flies around shit.

I was the prey of a lot of very hungry predators.

Within my first week, I had been hit on by over 30 guys and had been completely wooed by an Army Corporal. I soon discovered his fancy room fully equipped with a full double bed.

Lucky him, and lucky me.

'We're going this way, that way, forward, backward,

over the Irish sea, a bottle of rum to warm my tum, and that's the life for me' is all I recall singing while taking part in various drinking games on various nights.

There were lots of random parties and theme nights throughout my tour.

The main one being 'Fixmas'.

'Fixmas' was a fake Christmas day, it's so strange, I think it falls on 25th June, I can't quite remember, but we even had a complete roast dinner, and there were trees and decorations up all over the place.

I mean, it was bloody cold and snowy almost all the time, so you could easily be fooled.

A couple of months into my deployment, I embarked on a day trip of a lifetime.

A few of us got together and organised a helicopter flight to 'Volunteer Point', where the World's largest, accessible king penguin colony is.

We had to catch the chopper from Stanley.

This was the first time I had been to Stanley, the capital of the Falkland Islands.

It was a capital like no other.

No big city or town.

Just a few shack-like buildings, four pubs, three restaurants, and a town hall that serves as a post office.

The helicopter journey was incredible.

First time flying in one for all of us, plus the views were jaw-dropping.

We got dropped off and hiked over rocky terrain for around an hour to get to the colonies.

We made the mistake of having a picnic lunch on

route, and we were soon being hunted by massive, striated caracara and turkey vultures.

Both are equally as ugly and pretty terrifying up close. Google them!

The beach was a beautiful flat white stretch of sand, and there were penguins everywhere.

Hundreds and hundreds of them waddling across the shore.

It was an amazing sight.

People paid thousands to see spectacles like this.

I felt truly blessed to see cute, grey, fluffy balls of newly born king penguins hidden in the crowds.

An experience I won't ever forget.

I was provided with the opportunity to take part in the 'Liberation Day parade'. It is the national day of the Falkland Islands and commemorates the end of the occupation of the Falkland Island by Argentina in 1982.

I had to dig out my full number one uniform, white gloves, and all.

Can't say it was in the best of conditions after being stuck in a bag for weeks. A lot of ironing was required.

On the day, the sun was shining, and Christchurch cathedral, in Stanley, was illuminated against the clear blue sky.

I felt extremely privileged to be part of such a special occasion.

There is a famous whalebone archway near the cathedral. It was pretty much compulsory to have a photo taken underneath.

The parade went well. Luckily, I remembered how to march. It had been a while, and we all ended up drinking the evening away after.

Another achievement in the bag.

Well, actually, I lie, before the march, around 20 RAF, Army and Navy personal were chucked in a hanger and given a rifle for the parade, I could not for the life of me remember any arms drill, I was shocking, and, frankly, quite embarrassed.

Therefore, I wasn't given a weapon, and I was a glorified usher for all the important people who arrived in big black cars.

There were many more drunken nights in the bar between the excursions, events, and work, and many more men added to my tally.

I became quite close with one of the lads of my crew. Jason.

We had film nights together, took it in turns to give each other massages, and just genuinely got on well together. I'm not too sure why it didn't ever really develop into anything, to be honest.

He was one of the nice guys too.

So nice that one night he let one of his mates join in with us, and I don't mean just joining in with watching the film.

I was also one of the lucky fair few who got to witness the last flight of the iconic yellow Sea King, search and rescue helicopter.

A ceremony was held, and everyone on base attended. Its silhouette, and sound, seen and heard high above stormy seas and rocky coastlines, had been part and parcel of Falkland Islands life for generations of islanders, but the RAF's last Sea King made one final flight, albeit with a little help.

Underslung by the unmistakable Chinook, one of the RAF's decommissioned Sea King helicopters made its final flight across the Falklands before retiring.

It was a beautiful farewell, the sun was setting, and the skies were laced with pinks, purples, and oranges.

The Falkland Islands had an RAF Sea King search and rescue service since 1983.

It was now 2016.

While on tour, everyone is always on the countdown to go home.

On the fire section wall, there was a massive calendar. Each one of us had a 'mascot' which we would move daily, marking ourselves as one day closer to seeing our family and friends.

I genuinely enjoyed the bulk of my time in the Falklands, but that's because I got out and did things and made the most of it.

The people that moan about hating it are the ones who stay in their rooms and don't bother discovering everything the island has to offer or even the camp for that matter, and what's the point in that?

My name will forever remain on a golden plaque in the hallway of the fire section, along with a brick – it had become tradition over the years for every firefighter who had completed a tour in the Falklands to graffiti a brick in the crew room with their name and tour dates.

There were also some negatives to my time away, and I went through quite a bit of shit, not very pleasant shit, courtroom style shit, that left me exposed and feeling vulnerable and abused.

In actual fact, I was vulnerable and abused, but it's not something I want to delve into detail about.

That gave me an invitation to finish my deployment early. I didn't anyway, shit happens. That's life. We crack a smile and keep moving forward.

What's done is done, and we can't change the past.

Plus, if I left my tour early, that meant the bastard had won. He didn't own that kind of power; I wouldn't let him break me.

I'm a strong woman. Some women fear the fire, and some women simply become it.

6 BACKPACKING EUROPE, LOVE & OTHER DRUGS

"Travel opens your heart, broadens your mind, and fills your life with stories to tell."

I left the RAF at the end of 2017, and I served the minimum requirement asked of me, then decided to move on.

My life in the Military had many ups and downs, but without a doubt, it was one of the best things I ever could have done.

I learnt so much, grew so much as a person, experienced more things than you could imagine, and also made friends for life.

I'm still in a WhatsApp group with all the guys, and if I am ever feeling down, I just pop on there to see the GIFs and Memes being sent about.

I was, amazingly, granted four months of paid leave after ending my Military service.

Something that I would never get again in my life, and therefore I knew I had to do something amazing with my free time.

'Europe Inspired', by Topdeck.
A whole month of travelling, and camping, across Europe, living out of a backpack, and seeing hundreds of sites with a group of strangers from all over the World?
Sign me up, baby!

The following pieces of text are all true diary extracts from my mind-blowing European adventure. Twelve countries, 26 nights, and a mixture of bike, hike, boat, and coach tours in between.
Plus, a hell of a lot of boozing.

<u>24th August 2017</u>
"I haven't been everywhere, but it's on my list."

Well, it all begins.
Sat on the packed train from Northampton station to London Euston, ready for my 4-week adventure.
Really hope I have packed everything that I need.
Genuinely so excited to meet all my fellow travellers at 'Wombats' this afternoon.
Have to tackle a few of London's famous tubes first, though!

Arrived safe and sound at the hostel, not a bad place, but they are eight-man rooms with bunk beds, and there are already three other blokes set up in my room who aren't on my trip.
Not sure how I feel about leaving valuables in here.

First two people I met, who were on my trip, were Dan and Kieran.

Both from New Zealand.
I loved their accents!
There was something about Kieran as well, maybe his wiry ginger beard? Not sure, but I instantly liked him.

Little did I know that I would fall in love with him and end up going to New Zealand.

We went for a wander around London, then headed straight to Wetherspoons.
Standard. A few others joined us.
So far, everyone seemed lovely and a complete mix of ages and sexes and nationalities.
Some couples, but majority solo travellers.

Back at 'Wombats', the 'A team' was formed.
Me, Dan, Kieran, Nancy, and Grace.
Grace was from Australia and Nancy, the UK.
We all carried on drinking at the hostel bar till the early hours.
Kieran and I got together, hahaha, not even a day into the trip.
I sort of knew it would happen though, I can always tell.
No idea what time I went to bed.
Bloody steaming.

<u>25th August 2017</u>
"Lie begins at the end of your comfort zone."

It's 7.30 am, and I am absolutely hanging.

Woke up in Kieran's bunk.
Literally passed out there. Nothing happened.
Currently sat on a hot, stuffy coach on route to Paris, France.
Gunna be a long day of travelling.
Feels like I'm dying.
I need all the water in the World.

Well, we made it to France. I had a massive fat fry up on the ferry in the hope that it would cure my hangover.
It didn't.
We arrived at our hostel in Paris at around 5 pm, really nice location, right on the river, then we had the most beautiful gourmet picnic beneath the impressive Eiffel tower.
Bridges covered with lovelocks.
It was a pretty special evening, to be honest.
All of us are getting to know one another.
The 'A team' already sticking together like glue. I was mainly with Kieran.
The picnic was followed by another night of drinking.
Jagar bombs.
Vom.

26th August 2017
"Life is either a daring adventure or nothing."

Such an amazing day today.
Paris is so bloody beautiful.
Busy, very busy, but beautiful.
A few of us spent the morning at 'La Louvre', a

must-go, for anyone who visits Paris.
Had to tackle the crazy metro to get there, which was a whole different experience in itself, especially when the only French you speak is Bonjour and Une biere s'il vous plait.

Through the crowds at 'La Louvre', I managed to cast my eyes on the famous 'Mona Lisa'.
Can't say that I was wowed by it.
It's bloody tiny.

We visited 'Notre Dame', another incredible place, then Nancy and I took a scenic walk past the Eiffel tower, along the riverside, which soon changed into a relaxing boat tour down the river Seine.
So hot.
Very hungover again today, so I feel minging.

I was meant to go to a cabaret night, but I got stupidly drunk at the hostel, again, so I didn't make it out.
All of my group went.
I stayed at the bar.
Met some more new people, who were on trips of their own, got a right mix of mobile numbers and Facebook friends already.
A French guy and I were practicing yoga poses on the dance floor.
Legendary.

I officially love hostels.

Ok, so if you've never been to Paris. Go.
There is so much to see and do, not the cheapest of places but definitely worthwhile.
It's also a beautiful place to wander around, and they do the best croissants and coffee.
Oh, and get yourself a 'Paris pass' and 'Paris Museum pass'.

<u>27th August 2017</u>
"Remember that happiness is a way of travel, not a destination."

Got in at 6 am.
For fucks sake.
Stayed up drinking with Kieran again.
Was 4 am the day before and 2 am the day before that.
My poor little body.
How am I going to survive this trip?

We left the hotel at 8.30 am and set off to our next destination, the snowy Swiss Alps.
Really looking forward to this location.

Long, long day on the coach today.
We had to take turns to get up and say a little piece about ourselves.
I still don't know everyone's names.
My memory is shit.

Wow.
Ok, I am in love with Switzerland.
I want to move here, like right now.
It is officially the most beautiful place I have ever

been.

Currently driving through a small village called 'Lauterbrunnen', it is incredibly fairytale-like.

In the middle of a valley surrounded by mountains and waterfalls, the buildings are all wooden cabin-type places decorated with colourful hanging baskets and planters.

Just stunning.

We set up camp for the night right in the middle of the valley. I managed to get my tent up ok.

Mountain views right from my tent door, winning.

I was sensible tonight. I stayed on the water to give my poor liver a break!

Got to know Ella and Cherise better, love all these girls so much already.

Cherise is one of the bubbliest people I've ever met, and Ella is a fiery little redhead with great ambitions. She's a photographer, and her work is epic.

We set up camp at a site called 'Schutzenbach backpackers and camping/hostel'.

The facilities and bar there are the best.

The 'Stump bar' is a great place for socialising and testing out the famous ski shots.

The location is faultless.

The views and scenery are to die for.

If you are road-tripping Europe or looking at travelling on the cheap, unquestionably add this place to your list.

I will 100% be returned to Switzerland at some point in my life.

"In your wildest dreams, what would you do if you could do anything tomorrow?"

Today was such an amazing day, definitely the best day so far on this trip.
A load of us, I can't list everyone's names, took a train on the Jungfrau railway, up to the 'highest point in Europe'.
It was bloody freezing and completely layered with snow but so, so, so bloody beautiful.
The houses here are incredible.
Immaculate, pretty, and quaint.
We went to this ice palace, which was awesome, so many photos were taken.
Lots of ice sculptures and caves and tunnels to explore.
An incredibly impressive place, to be honest.

Everyone struggled a little bit at the top of the mountain due to vertigo.
All the girls got topless, and all the lads completely butt naked, because, you know, why the hell not.
Such good fun and the pictures are epic, next Facebook banner pic for sure.
Don't even know these people, and I've seen their tits and dicks already.
We were out all day until we got the scenic train back down at around 4 pm.

I was going to go for a run once we got back but

*ended up in the bar drinking my body weight in gin
and ski shots.*
Ski shots are messy!
Hey ho, everyone was out and having a good time.
It really was an amazing day all round.
Who needs to run anyway!?
*Chantel and Trav, one of the New Zealand couples,
are so bloody lovely and very much loved up. It's
super cute.*
*Honestly couldn't be making this trip with a better
bunch of people.*

29th August 2017
*"A mind that is stretched by a new experience can never go
back to its old dimensions."*

Fuck. I really need to stop all this drinking.
So bloody rough this morning.

On route to pizza and pasta country, Italy, today.
*We stopped off at Pisa for a couple of hours, really
busy, but another amazing place.*
Got some compulsory leaning tower of Pisa photos.

*We then headed off to Florence. The drive there
was probably the most scenic to date.*
*We pitched up our tents at the most awkward,
sloped, rocky, campsite then went on a sunset
walking tour of the city before going for dinner.*
It was incredible.
Such amazing views and the colours of the sky were

utterly breathtaking.

Never eaten so much pasta in my life. The portion sizes were mammoth but delicious.
Food babies all around.
Thank God for all these walking tours.

A few of us girls, sensibly, decided against a night on the piss and went to get gelato instead, over one hundred flavours to choose from.
Heaven.

Mel is a total legend, and I love her. She's another Kiwi. Loads of Kiwis and Aussies on this trip.

Florence was one of my favourite places on the whole trip, everything about it, and one of the cheapest places in Italy.
If you like art, culture, history, or cathedrals, I highly recommend going.

30th August 2017
"Man cannot discover new oceans unless he dares to lose sight of the shore."

Up bright and early for a full guided tour of the stunning Florence.
I'll be returning to Italy for sure. It's all just beautiful.

Bloody scorching today. That sun is hot, hot, hot.

Saw all the main sites, lots of museums and art

galleries.

The city is known for its culture, art, and architecture. Some really quirky-looking buildings.
Had lunch in a cute little café before jumping back on the coach to Rome.

No chill out time once we arrived at Rome, straight out for a three-hour walking tour. In the dark.
Saw so much, though, and to be honest, everything looked so nice, all lit up at night.
Halfway through, we stopped for dinner at the most amazing pizzeria.
More gelato followed the pizza.
I had lemon, kiwi, and pistachio.
I've surely gained about four stones already while being away.

The iconic Colosseum, and all the surrounding ancient ruins, were epic to see, especially at night when majority of the tourists weren't out.
A lot bigger than I thought too.

The Trevi fountain was heaving, but we all got to throw a coin in.

Had the stressful experience of the Italian metro back to our campsite.
Best campsite yet though, there is a swimming pool!
And shops, plus we have wooden cabins rather than tents.
Luxury.

It was 10 pm by the time we had sorted out all of our crap, but there was a big 'Toga party' happening on-site. Obviously, we couldn't miss that.

Wrapped up in bedsheets and make-do belts, we hit the party. Well, most of us did anyway. Some opted for an early night.

For once, I didn't get foolishly drunk, just had a few gins. The party ended shortly after midnight, but I was out until 3 am.
Kieran and I spent those few after-party hours walking and talking.
Something is going on between us now.
He is so much younger than me, I need to remember that, but I do really like him, not my usual type at all.

Alarm set for 6 am.
Lovely.

<u>31st August 2017</u>
"Travelling tends to magnify all human emotions."

Today was my new favourite day.
Absolutely loved it.
Got up super early to visit the home of the Pope, the Vatican City.
It's enormous, well actually it's the smallest country in the World, but I didn't realise that it was even a country or even a separate place from Rome until visiting.
It has its own police, number plates, completely

separate from everywhere else.
*We visited all the top sites, including St Peter's
Basilica, St Peters square, and the Sistine Chapel.*
No words can really describe the Sistine Chapel.
It was unbelievably breathtaking.
It completely overwhelmed me, and I actually cried.
*It was really odd, I walked in, deadly silence as you
aren't allowed to talk, and I was instantly hit with a
wave of emotion.*
I'm not even religious.
*One of the other girls, Kat, was exactly the same, so
I didn't feel silly.*
*I think everyone must pay a visit there at least once
in their lives.*

The Vatican City made me feel emotions I'd never
felt before.
I'm not religious or spiritual or anything like that at
all, yet when I walked into the Sistine Chapel, I felt
something, I can't explain it, but I instantly got
goosebumps and wanted to cry.
It's such a special, beautiful place.

*All of us girls, who now feel like sisters, went off
for a beautiful prosecco lunch at a gorgeous
restaurant after our tour, then tackled two metros
and a bus to get back to camp.*

Straight in the swimming pool.

*Most of the guys were already there, having
beers and chilling.*
After a hot, sunny few days, the pool was a

Godsend. Plus, it was nice to get in the bikini and have a bit of a sunbathe too!

Dinner was at 8 pm. Liz, one of our tour leaders and the crew chef, did a great job tonight, a lovely risotto.
However, everyone was on their first cocktail bucket (and I mean big bucket!) by this point, so nobody bothered about eating.
Everyone seemed in such good spirits tonight, but we are losing eight people off the trip from here, which is sad.
I'll miss Cherise, Kat, and Myriam for sure.

More buckets, more shots.

11.30 pm and I went to bed.
Kieran was so bloody drunk.
He came knocking on my door four times, which the girls I'm sharing with weren't too happy about.
I only answered twice as I was getting pissed off.
Drunks really are so irritating when you're not steaming yourself – now I know how people see me!

Missing the gym.
Feel minging.
Only been away just over a week. Another three to go yet.
Going to be alright, fatty.

Rome was full of haunting ruins, vibrant street life, and awe-inspiring art.
Another must-go place for anyone visiting Italy.

Quite expensive though, so remember that.

"You don't have to be rich to travel well."

Woke up this morning to pissing down rain.
Not ideal, but I guess I can't complain as I've had fantastic weather up until now.
Had brekkie and jumped on the coach at 8 am, next stop Venice.
Said goodbye to the few that left us, down to 30 now, and more to leave next week.
It's so sad, everyone is like family now, but only a certain few are making the full trip.
Kieran is one of them.

We stopped off at Verona for a couple of hours on route.
Undeniably beautiful little place, I saw Juliet's balcony (from Romeo and Juliet), and I posted a letter to her on the wall – apparently, they come true.
We will see.

Go to Verona!! That is all.

We arrived in Venice to massive thunderstorms and golf ball-sized hailstones.
Therefore, we all upgraded our accommodation from tents to cabins.
A masquerade ball was happening on site, but everyone was so knackered, we all got an early night.

109

In bed by a very respectable 11 pm.

2nd September 2017
"Oh, the places you'll go."

This morning, after breakfast, we had a walking tour of Venice and a lace workshop talk.
Venice is amazing.
So pretty, and the way all the canals spiral through the streets is fascinating.
There are over four hundred bridges.
No cars exist. You have to rely on boats and your trusty feet.

Kieran, Dan, Grace, Nancy, and I hired a gondola – one of those narrow canal boats with an Italian to 'drive' you along.
It was bloody awesome, so glad we did it.
Definitely the best way to see Venice and a super relaxing experience.

The gondola ride wasn't cheap by any means, but if you do visit the incredible Venice, I feel you should experience it the way the locals do; you won't regret it, and you can take the most wonderful photos from the canal.
I loved Venice and will undoubtedly go back.
Getting up for sunrise is a must.

The whole crew met for our last Italian meal, which was pizza.

We carried on exploring after, and I discovered

the most amazing little book shop.
'Libreria Acqua Alta'.
The steps were creatively formed with books.
I believe it is actually known as one of the World's
most beautiful bookshops, and I could definitely see
why.

Google this place, and you'll see why I fell in love
with it. Topdeck used a photo of me, sat on the
books, on their website for a while.
Famous.

Tonight, on camp, was a traffic light party. I
didn't even know what this was at first, but
basically, you have to wear red if you're taken,
green if you're single and yellow means it's
complicated.
I wore green.

Jeez, what a night.
Everything that could happen happened.
I had a whole bottle of prosecco as my pre-drink.
Met a guy at the bar, all over each other, so didn't
take long before we went back to his bunk.
Kieran saw everything.

So much tequila, but so much fun dancing.

When the party was over, Kieran came to speak
to me. He told me how much he liked me. He
doesn't care what I've done and how he hasn't felt
like this about anyone in ages.
I was quite blunt with him and told him that I do

like him, but that's it. It doesn't go any further.
He walked me back to my cabin, where another lad
tried it on with me.
They got in a fight, Kieran started it, security got
involved, and we all got escorted to bed.
Not the best ending to the evening.

3rd September 2017
"Just go, go see all the beauty in the World."

Not fresh at all this morning. This is the worst
I've felt, ever.
So tired, but man, what a night.
Everyone seems to have stories to tell.

On route to Pag Island today.

Stopped in Slovenia for a few hours, another
beautiful place, reminds me of Switzerland.

As we crossed the border into Croatia, I could
instantly tell that it was going to be yet another
gorgeous place, and it is so hot and sunny.
Bliss.

Had to jump on a short ferry journey across to
Pag island, where we located our campsite.
The site is right on the beach, literally pitched upon
the golden sand.
How amazing is this!?
The sea is crystal clear, and the skies pure blue.

A few of my fellow travellers headed into town for the night. I chose to take a sunset beach stroll and grab an early night.

"Collect moments, not things."

I got up early to catch the sunrise and have a yoga session on the beach.
It was so peaceful. Everyone else still asleep.
Most beautiful scenery and colours.
Worth getting up early for sure.
Makes you feel so alive.

We had an all-day boat party with all-inclusive drinks.
Dangerous.
Home brewed wine. Strong as fuck and tasted vile.
The boat stopped every now and again so we could have swimming breaks. Some of the lads swam out to cliffs and jumped off them.
We even got to try fishing, which was pretty cool.

Lovely sunny day. The tan is coming along nicely.

The boat party ended.
Majority of people were steaming, and on the way back to camp, the coach broke down, so we had to take it in turns to get a six-man shuttle bus.
I cracked open another bottle of prosecco once we were back.
Wasn't really feeling it, though.

Nancy and Kieran are all cosy together, cuddling and holding hands. What the hell is going on there? Really got to me for some reason. Enough to make me go crying to Ella about it.

I thought I'd get an early night, but that didn't go to plan.

Had the mother of all spiders in my tent, and it had a bundle of babies in the sack on its back.

Jordan and Tom came to my rescue. Well, they tried but ended up breaking the sack of babies, so I had hundreds of spiders now in the tent. They were literally everywhere.

Worst nightmare.

Tom also found a spider in his tent, so we opted to sleep under the coach. However, we thought we should man up, so we went back to our tents.

I didn't sleep, obviously.

It's about 3 am, and there's now these weird millipedes everywhere, and ants, so many bloody ants, oh and bats.

Like a fucking jungle out there.

Take spider repellent or something if you camp here. I don't think spider repellent is even a thing, though, so grab some conkers or make a bomb.

<u>5th September 2017</u>
"Live while you're alive."

Woke up at 7.30 am to a lizard in my tent. Fantastic.

Breakfast isn't until 9 am, so going to go for a little

wander down the beach.

Ended up skinny dipping.
Was amazing, actually. Super refreshing and very liberating.
After a yummy French toast breakfast, the girls and I got a taxi into town.
The lads all hired scooters for the day.
We explored the pretty little seaside town, then found a perfect spot on the beach, next to a beach bar, complete with hammocks and loungers.
Sheer bliss.
Wasn't even 11 am but we hit the cocktails straight away.
I was on my all-time favourites, Pina Colada.
Living my best life right now.

So nice to sunbathe and have a proper swim in the sea, the waters are perfectly clear here, so many fish to watch.
We went to a place called 'Moby Dicks' for lunch. I was super adventurous for once and ordered Shark! Was really, really good, similar to Swordfish but a bit meatier.
More cocktails went down. Grace and Ella fucked. They are such lightweights. It's so funny.
They are super young, though, to be fair.
It was nice to get to know Chantal a bit more, she's lovely, and she and Trav are just the perfect couple.

Brought a new playsuit for our five-course boat meal in Budapest on Thursday, then we went back to the beach for a final hour of sunbathing and more cocktails, of course.

Back at camp, I chose to drink no more and went for another walk down the beach.
Nancy and Kieran were all over each other again, so I didn't want to be there to watch.

It was a full moon, so the reflections on the water looked epic.

Don't know why the Kieran thing is getting to me so much, maybe I'll speak to him tomorrow when we are both sober.

Went to bed at 10 pm after a heart-to-heart with Tom. He is such a lovely guy, but literally ten years younger than me.

Think the group will mix up a lot once we lose the next ten in Budapest.
All the 'clicks' will be lost.

<u>6th September 2017</u>
"There's no time to be bored in a world so beautiful."

Bloody early. Got up this morning. 5.30 am.
I was still one of the first to have my tent and bag packed up, even though I didn't have a tent partner to help me. I did good.
Breakfast and coffee while the hazy sun rose.
I'll miss Croatia, but not the campsite and all its creepy crawlies.

Over eight hours of driving to be done today.

Been over two weeks now since I've properly trained, the belly is feeling the effects. I feel gross, but not much I can do about it. Been on a couple of runs and done the odd yoga session, but that's it, other than all the walking.

As soon as we arrived in Budapest, we headed off on a short tour, and all the major sites were pointed out to us, so we knew where to go on our free day tomorrow.

Setting up tents in the dark wasn't exactly a fun task, but once done, we went to the most amazing burger bar for dinner, had to get an old school tram to get into the city.
Our tour leaders took us to this weird but astonishing club, which was basically a converted apartment block. Therefore, soooo many different rooms to choose from.
It was amazing!
The cocktails were bloody strong.
I danced the night away with Mel and Ella.
It was a great night.

<u>7th September 2017</u>
"Love is the food of life, and travel is dessert."

Woke up early, and surprisingly, wasn't feeling too rough, so I went for a run, and did yoga, feel so much better for it.

Had a free day today.

Me, Ella, Mel, Grace, and Nancy, went and explored beautiful Budapest.

We climbed up to the top of St Stephens Basilica.

Views were incredible, bloody high, though, and a hell of a lot of steps.

Then we went on to Europe's biggest synagogue, the 'Dohany street synagogue'.

The exterior was impressive enough, but the interior was absolutely breathtaking.

Some parts were incredibly upsetting, as the complex houses a hero's temple and a graveyard.

The tree of life, or the weeping willow, is a beautiful monument in memory of the 600,000 Jews who were murdered by the German Nazis.

Gives you goosebumps.

Coffee and pancakes lined our bellies as we continued walking and exploring.

So much to see here.

Had a stupidly late lunch at this enormous food market.

Had the 'World's biggest quesadilla'.

Definitely earnt the fatty title.

Back at camp, we all got dolled up for our dinner and drinks cruise.

Budapest looks stunning at night, especially the huge Parliament buildings that overlook the river.

Mel and I got pretty wasted. I get on so well with her, she's great.

Two bottles of wine and a bottle of prosecco down before we had even eaten.
Dinner was an enormous buffet laid out down the centre of the boat.
Was a lot to try, no idea what some of the things even were.

I 'led' half the group to a club, once we had docked, I was bloody steaming, and fuck knows where I was even going. I did find a club, though.

Stopped for a wee behind a car, at least I thought I was behind a car, but I certainly wasn't hidden at all.

Had such a laugh, drinking and dancing all night.
Not sure what time we left; it was pretty late, though. Kieran came back to my tent for a chat, and he told me that I really hurt him when I got with that lad the other night and how Nancy had been his rock.
Blah, blah, blah.
We agreed to start afresh.
I don't even know how I feel or what I want, plus the trip will be over in a couple weeks.

One of the most photogenic cities in Europe is Budapest.
Dramatic skylines, full of history, lots of churches, bridges, museums, and one of the cheapest destinations I visited on the trip.

8th September 2017

"Work, save, travel, repeat."

Two hours sleep, for fucks sake.
Feeling super rough and so, so tired.
Very much looking forward to staying in a hostel,
rather than a tent, tonight.
Up at 6 am to pack away the tents and shit.
Eleven others left us here, including Nancy, Ella,
Lucy, and Scott, and Joe and Courtney.
Only 19 left now, going to be strange with such a
small group.

On route to Krakow, Poland, today.

Hostel is pretty decent, 6 per room, and it has a
comfy bunk bed with duvets.
Big communal room too.
We dumped our bags then headed out on the
cobbled streets for a walking tour around the old
town, which was declared the first UNESCO World
Heritage site in the World.
Then we mooched around the 'Wawel Royal castle'.
An incredibly beautiful place is Krakow.
One of my new favourites.

Wow, it is so, so cheap!!

There's a bar crawl going on tonight, so we are
now sat pre-drinking vodka at the hostel.
First bar was all you can drink for an hour, insane.
So, everyone got happily steaming there, for free.

I and Kieran are on good terms again now and stayed with each other the whole night.

Still not sure what is going on with us.

Anyway, lots of drinking and dancing in that first bar. In the second bar, we had vodka literally poured down our throats upon arrival.

I don't recall too much after that, lots of blank patches. I do remember being sat in MacDonald's munching a cheeseburger.

I stayed in Kieran's bed.

Can't believe we still haven't slept with each other yet. I'm so confused with myself and the situation.

9th September 2017
"All good things are wild and free."

Dying.

Everyone is just as rough.

Brilliant night though.

Free day to explore today, I headed off out with Mel and Grace.

I am so in love with Krakow.

We went to the top of St Marys Basilica, inside the beautiful Wawel Cathedral, and wandered back around the castle.

After a delicious lunch of meaty dumplings, we perused around the Jewish quarters before taking a leisurely stroll by the river.

Mel is so hanging!

Had a 2-hour nap back at the hostel, then the whole group explored the 'underground museums', which are located below the main square.

Pretty awesome, to be honest. You wouldn't even know it existed.

No wild partying tonight, all of us stayed in and had an early night.

Bed is amazing.

I never even considered visiting Krakow or Poland before, but as soon as we arrived, I knew I wanted to go back.
It is super cheap, so much to see and do, and a gorgeous, friendly place.
Everyone needs to give it a visit. Seriously, it is completely underrated.

10th September 2017
"Dare to live the life you've always wanted."

Super early wake up again.
Bloody 5.30 am. Eugh. At least I got more than 4 hours sleep for once, think I got a full 6.

The morning was spent at Auschwitz.
So, so, bloody emotional.
I really struggled to hold it all together. To be honest, I broke down a few times.
We saw all the shoes, clothes, and even the hair, of everyone that died there.
Over 1.1 million people lost their lives at Auschwitz, including a lot of children.
We also got to go inside the gas chamber, that wasn't nice at all, really eery

Weird experience. Some people couldn't even go in.

Need to watch a funny movie or something after that visit.

We have now arrived in Prague, setting up our tents and having dinner.

We were due to go on a walking tour of the city, but as we arrived at the campsite much later than planned, it has been scrapped until the morning.

The group sat around the cook tent, having a few beers and chilling.

I headed off to my tent early, Kieran came with me. We had sex for the first time. Not the most comfortable, on a rocky floor with a deflated mattress mind. It was a long time coming, really.

Can't sleep at all, used to having the tent to myself. He is taking up all of it.

I'm fucking freezing, and it's so bloody cold.

<u>11th September 2017</u>
"Life is a one-time offer. Use it well."

Ok, so today was one of my favourite mornings ever.

Me, James, and Kieran got up at 5 am to go and watch the sunrise at Charles bridge.

Just one metro to catch, which was easy enough.

Massive, beautiful, medieval bridge.

So peaceful and quiet.

A bride and groom photoshoot was taking place at

the opposite end of the bridge. They both looked amazing.

The sun rose and illuminated the bridge and the river with a golden glow. It was, without a doubt, one of the finest sunrises I have seen.

I am so glad the boys actually got up to come with me.

Such an amazing start to the day.

Sunrise has always been my favourite time of day. Was made more special by sharing this one with Kieran too.

We made it back to camp in time for breakfast, thankfully, as I was starving.

Our walking tour began soon after.

Prague really is another stunning place.

The buildings are beautiful. Very elegant.

We took some awesome group photos in front of the 'John Lennon' wall. It was on my list of things to see in Prague.

I used my free time to head up to Prague Castle to witness the changing of the guards, was rather cool to watch, I suppose, but I wasn't blown away by it.

Afterwards, Mel, Grace, Chantel, Trav, Kieran, Jay, Dan, and I discovered a unique pub.

The place was surrounded by a miniature railway. Our drinks, and food, were delivered by trains. It was awesome.

Tonight was spent having a five-course medieval

dinner. The restaurant was basically a cave, never been anywhere like it.
Not everyone came. The couples were there, so were me, Mel, and Grace.
It was a brilliant evening.
Unlimited wine and beer, with the most incredible entertainment.
Belly dancing, swordfights, fire dancing, plus a band of topless men, so, can't complain.
The wine went down too well, especially with Mel and me.

After the meal, we met the rest of the gang at a dance bar. Night on the pole and dancing like dick heads was great fun.

Bloody freezing in my tent again tonight, looking forward to our next stop, Berlin, when we are back in a hostel.
My back is fucked from sleeping on the floor.

Another severely underrated place.
Prague is up there in my top ten countries.
It is stunning, day and night.
Anyone who goes must visit the 'Astronomical clock', Old town square, and the 'John Lennon' wall.
The place is jam packed with history, art and culture.
Also, be sure to get up for sunrise and head to the bridge.
It's magical.

<u>12th September 2017</u>
"Life is short, and the World is wide."

I am so tired this morning. Desperate for a good night's sleep.

We left Prague at 9 am to head for Germany. Only a week left of this trip now. It's insane, gone so quickly. Don't want to go home.

Spoke to Mum and Dad, nothing to report from them. Anna was at work, so I didn't get the chance to say hello to her.

We stopped off at Dresden for a leg stretch and a wander around. Nice little place, lots of interesting-looking buildings.
I grabbed a greasy 'Bratwurst' sausage and chips for my lunch, followed by a random chocolate-covered banana on a stick.

I, Mel, and Grace have formed such a close little bond over the last few days. It's lovely.

Another 2 hours on the bus, then we parked up outside the hostel in Berlin.
So many sites to see here, going to be a busy couple of days trying to see it all, and I want to visit it all.

We have another bar crawl tomorrow night, eugh, don't think my body can do it.
Honestly cannot wait to be back in the gym and back to eating clean and not drinking every bloody day.

Kieran just asked me out to dinner when we get

to Copenhagen. Obviously, I said yes.

I haven't been on a date in over five years.

Will be odd, but I guess I've been spending so much time with him already that it won't make much difference.

Not sure what will happen when we get back to London. He is staying in the UK until October, and then he will fly all the way back to NZ.

Fuck knows. Doubt anything further will happen.

We'll be too far apart for anything to happen anyway.

This Berlin hostel is amazing.

Indoor pool, en-suites, common rooms, and the funkiest interior.

It's epic, and I can't wait to be in that bed, under that duvet later.

I went out for a run down the East side gallery to see the graffiti walls, then back across on the other side of the river.

Felt good.

The air stinks of weed here.

My phones fucked. Full-on frozen.

Won't turn off or on or anything.

Brilliant.

Have to wait for the battery to die and hope for the best.

Mum and Dad will worry if I don't get in touch again soon.

Felt incredible to have a nice, long, hot shower, then curl up in the comfiest bed.

I am so glad I skipped going to the bar tonight.
This wins.

13th September 2017
"Escape the ordinary."

Oh my God. Had the best night's sleep. Feel amazing about it too. So, so good to be back in a bed!

There was a walking tour arranged for after breakfast, but I, Mel, and Grace did our own thing. This seems to be becoming the norm now.
Was pissing down all morning.
And cold.
We got bloody drenched, was so much fun though, we laughed till we cried.
We started our own little tour at the 'Reichstag' Parliament buildings, then strolled through a pretty park to get to the famous archways, the 'Brandenburg Gate', before passing through 'Museum Island' to the glorious Berlin Cathedral, which was just stunning.

Had the most delicious hot chocolate at the top of the television tower, the 360° views were incredible.
Was nice to be dry and warm for a short period of time.
Taste buds satisfied, we headed to this weird memorial for murdered Jews, also known as the 'Holocaust memorial'. Lots of different-sized blocks laid out in a maze-like format, every block represented a life.

Creepy, really, but was good to see.

The rain finally stopped, and we walked to 'Checkpoint Charlie', which is where the divide for the American sector was, and basically the border crossing between East and West Berlin during the cold war.
Men were dressed as guards, and there was a small museum about the history of it all, definitely worth a visit.

A bottle of prosecco downed before I met the rest of the group for our pre-bar crawl dinner.
I wasn't very hungry but still smashed a whole pizza, along with another bottle of plonk.
Fucked by the time the bar crawl and night tour even started.

I don't really remember much of the night, to be honest. I remember crying to Kieran, telling him that I don't want to say goodbye to him – what a girl.
Also, remember I and Mel drunk weeing together, then sitting on a curb eating some greasy take away food.

Back at the hostel, Kieran told me that he wants to spend every last minute he has in the UK with me and how he has never felt like this for anyone before.
Bless him.
I do really like him but, not going to allow myself to get too involved as it can't last.

He lives on the other side of the World, for fucks sake.

It's probably just a little tour romance anyway.

Berlin undeniably had the most landmarks and historical buildings. You need two or three days minimum to be able to see everything.
I mean, it is the largest city in Germany, and very popular, so very busy, but worth tackling the crowds for sure.

<u>14th September 2017</u>
"Escape the ordinary."

Eugh.
Very rough.
Some of the lads didn't get in until 6 am.
After breakfast, we all piled back on the coach, ready for our next destination, Copenhagen.
Been told it's freezing there at the moment, brilliant, really looking forward to sleeping in a tent again.
Not.

Can't believe there are only two more places left after Copenhagen.
Flown by.
Really don't want it to be over.

We had to take a short ferry crossing over to Denmark, then had a further 2 hours of driving until we reached our campsite.
It was chucking it down when we arrived, and no one wanted to set up tents, so we took a driving tour around the city until it eased off.

I may have napped a little on the bus.

One of our leaders took us to this weird drug marketplace, sellers lined all down the streets, and it bloody stank of weed.
Strange place indeed.
And it's legal.

Back to camp to complete darkness, so setting up tents was a challenge. Kieran helped me with mine, thankfully.
Bless him.

Weather still proper shit, so going to bed. It's only 10 pm, but fuck it.

<u>15th September 2017</u>
"Twenty years from now, you will be more disappointed by the things you didn't do than by the ones you did do."

Had a really shitty night's sleep.
Was so cold and rainy all night.

Another free day today. Think Mel, Grace, and I have a whole list of places we want to go and things we want to see!
Can't wait, been looking forward to being here.
Plus, the sun is shining.

Wow, feel knackered. We saw so much today.
Started with climbing to the top of 'Church of Our Saviour', tiny, narrow, spiral staircase and so bloody windy on the way up. Worth it for the

panoramic views though, they were incredible.
Could see for miles and miles, so glad it was a clear day.

We then headed back to the druggy place, which we discovered was called 'Christiana', we were told there was some Windmill thing there, but we never found it. We did find most of the boys there, at the stalls, buying weed.
Standard.

The streets are literally full of famous landmarks and buildings, we passed the stock exchange, the Palace, the Opera House, and that's just to name a few.
One of my favourite parts of today was the food market. It was enormous, and so many different stalls. We settled for tacos, followed by cheesecake. Was so dam good.

The colourful little houses that line the canals and the 17th-century waterfront are stunning, so vivid, and happy.
I loved them.
Just sitting on the canal side, people watched, made me smile from ear to ear.
Copenhagen has completely stolen my heart.

It started to rain again, we bumped into Kieran, so I went off with him for a bit.
We explored the castle and had a lovely, wet walk around the spectacular botanical gardens, and then he took me to dinner.
My first date in forever.
He took me to this beautiful little place right by the

canal.

It was perfect.

I did have a really nice time, but still just confused with it all, and what I want, what he wants, blah, blah, blah.

Had a few drinks with the gang back at camp before heading to my tent, last night of camping, hostels for the rest of the trip after this.

Kieran came in to tell me what a good evening he had with me and that he's so glad he met me.

I just wanted to sleep, to be honest, but he had other ideas, and my PJs were soon back off.

Again, I had never considered visiting Copenhagen before, but so glad we went there.

It's packed with cute little cafes, shops, and restaurants. It's described on Wikipedia as 'Friendly old girl of a town', which does sum it up perfectly.

Also known as the happiest city in the World, and if you take a trip there, you'll see why.

16th September 2017

"Wherever you go becomes part of you somehow."

I'm cold, damp, tired, and moody.

Another rubbish night's sleep. So glad there's no more camping now.

Get me back to a bed.

Next stop, Hungary.

So back to Germany on the bus, we go.

'I've been up all night, no sleep, cause I feel like I'm always dreaming' became the song of our trip,

so we were all forever singing it.
I just want to keep travelling. I genuinely don't want
to go back to a normal, shitty, boring life.
If I had more money, I would absolutely take a few
more months out to see the World.

We arrived at our hostel, pissing down with rain
once again, and Hamburg didn't seem like it had
too much to offer, plus it was only really a stopover
point, so we stayed in for the night.
There was a bar on-site, Mel and I got through
two bottles of prosecco and half a bottle of absinthe
in just a few hours.
Thinking about it now makes me feel sick.
Grace got smashed on a bottle of vodka.
Mel then disappeared with our bus driver.
Ha, ha, ha, ha God, I love that girl.

<u>17th September 2017</u>
"You'll never know until you go."

Off to Amsterdam, in the Netherlands, we go.
Last stop before heading back to London
On route to our hostel, we stopped at a farm to see
how cheese and clogs were produced, which was
pretty fascinating.
How ugly are clogs, though!?

The houses here are ridiculous.
Bloody massive, with humongous gardens that
house pools and gyms.
Insane.

I wasn't expecting this here at all.
Also, Amsterdam is so, so pretty.

Well, this evening was an experience.
While on a walking tour, a few of us got hash brownies from a local store.
Never again, I felt so, so fucked. Grace and Chantal were just as bad.
The guy in the shop did say to only have a tiny bit if you haven't done it before, but stupidly, I had over half.
I thought I was constantly walking on a slope and holding on to a rope to help me.
At one point, I was crawling on the floor. What a twat!

We went to a bloody live sex show while we were all fucked.
I was about 2 feet away from the stage.
Such a weird encounter. A couple was literally banging right in front of us.
Kieran, Tom, and Trav had to go up on stage and eat a banana out of the woman's pussy.
Brett, bless him, got dragged up too. It was so, so funny to watch. He was so nervous and awkward
Later in the night, he spewed everywhere, another one that couldn't handle the brownie.
I couldn't even string a sentence together.
Chantal couldn't walk.
Grace was crying.
We were a mess.
I don't even know how we made it back to the hostel. The other hardcorers carried on to a bar.
I remember just staring at a woman in the Red-light

district while she was dancing in her box.

I passed out at 10.30 pm.

<u>18th September 2017</u>
"People don't take trips. Trips take people."

Up bright and early for a bike tour around Amsterdam. I surprisingly feel ok, which I was not expecting at all.
Quite looking forward to today, actually.

I loved the tour.
We went all over.
Through this beautiful park, past the famous Amsterdam sign, past Ann Franks house, the Opera House, Van Gogh Museum, and through the Red-light district.
Had such a laugh as well, everyone having a good time and enjoying the sites.
Took some epic photos.

Post cycle coffee and cake with Mel and Gracey at this quirky street café before going to the sex museum.
As you can imagine, just full of cocks and tits.
We were laughing like teenagers.
Great fun, though.
The girls and I carried on walking and exploring, taking in the scenic bridges and flowers that seemed to be everywhere.
Honestly, I never knew Amsterdam was so beautiful, would 100% come back.

Got our full-on tourist photos at the Amsterdam sign, then headed back to the hostel to get ready for our final meal and have pre-drinks.
Mel and I had two bottles of prosecco before going out. No surprise there, really.

A three-story, floating Chinese restaurant awaited us.
It looked mega, and the views were wowing.
The food was really nice, but not enough of it for my liking.
Had another two bottles of wine with dinner.
Pretty pissed before we left for the bar crawl.
Yeah, another bar crawl.
It was such a decent night, though, laughing and dancing away with each other
The NZ trio, James, Jordan, and Ben, are staying on in Amsterdam, so it was goodbye to them, as we would be leaving early in the morning.
Sad times, they are good lads.
Three bars later and I was ready to go to bed.

Can't believe this is the last night. I feel really upset about it. Don't want it to end.
I love these guys and girls so much.
I'm going to have a drunken cry under my duvet.

I always thought of Amsterdam as prostitutes and drugs.
But how wrong was I?
I mean, yes, there is the red-light district, but it is nothing like I imagined, so do not let that put you off. It's very 'classy'. There aren't women stood on street

corners. They are in immaculate glass boxes in stylish underwear.

It's such a colourful and pretty city. Very clean and tidy.

Once again, lots to see and do.

I recommend a bike tour. It's the best way to see Amsterdam.

19th September 2017
"It's not what you look at that matters. It's how you feel."

No. I will not accept this. It's my last day with this lot. It's like 5 am, and we are already on the bus. Hanging and exhausted.
Got a long day of travelling ahead.

I got upset on the bus and again on the ferry about leaving Kieran. He is in the UK for a few more weeks yet, so I said I would go to London, or he can come to Northampton.

Well, we got back to Wombats in London.
Toughest day ever.
Saying goodbye was so fucking hard.
Even more so to Mel and Grace.
Lots of cuddles and lots of tears.
I really do hope I get to see some of these amazing people again, been the most incredible month, and we've experienced so much together.
Kieran had to get one of the same tubes as me, so we stayed a bit longer together, but when I had to jump off that tube, the tears were never-ending.
I will definitely see him before he goes home.

The train pulled up in Northampton, and both Mum and Dad were there to greet me. It was nice to see them, but I was so tired, I just wanted to go to bed, so we got home. I showed them my photos then I hit the sack.

So good to be back in a proper bed, in a room on my own, though.

Just one day after being home, I was back at the train station and jumping on a train to London.

Mum said, 'You go travelling round Europe and come back with a bloody Kiwi'.

Still makes me laugh.

I ended up staying at Kieran's cousin's house for almost two weeks.

Kieran and I explored London like tourists. We went to Richmond Park, Camden Market, Regents Park, Hyde Park, Tower bridge... we walked over 15km one day.

It was great, to be honest.

He went back to New Zealand in October, and I started a new job with Thames Valley Police as a facial imaging officer.

I was great at that job.

We worked a long-distance relationship, which was bloody tough, especially with the time differences, but we managed it.

By this point, we had both already said, 'I love you'.

Kieran invited me to spend Christmas with him and his family. I had to decline. After everything I went through in Canada, I just couldn't do it to myself.

He reinvited me for New year.
So, there I was, sat on my laptop, and £1387 later, I'd bought a plane ticket to the other side of the World.

Bloody expensive, I know.
What are credit cards for, eh!?

7 ROAD-TRIPPING NEW ZEALAND, TWICE

"If it excites you and scares you, at the same time, it probably means you should do it."

Wednesday 27th December 2017, and Mum and Dad, were, once again, dropping me off at terminal three, Heathrow airport, ready for me to embark on my longest flight yet.
29 hours.

London → Dubai → Melbourne → Christchurch

It wasn't actually half as bad as it sounds.
I flew with 'Qantas airlines', and I couldn't fault the service at all.
Super comfy seats, lots of films, and meals every few hours, plus free drinks.
They were needed.
I did panic slightly when I landed in Melbourne as I didn't have any stopover time and had to run to board my next plane. I was shitting myself, to be fair.
I was one of the last on.

I also had an anxiety attack over my luggage at this point. I mean, the last time I had seen it was over 20 hours prior. It could have ended up anywhere in the World, and luckily, it did arrive in Christchurch shortly after me.

Kieran was waiting for me with open arms in arrivals.
It was an emotional reunion and quite weird. I hadn't seen him in over two months.
I was bloody knackered and really needed a shower, but rather than chilling, Kieran took me on a long hike up the 'Port hills'. The views were breathtaking and well worth the climb.
He knew I was a fan of views.
I could see the whole of Christchurch; the landscape was stunning.
New Zealand quickly became my favourite country.

My first couple of days were spent getting over my jet lag and exploring the local area.
I was staying in the family home in a small town called Woodend, located about 25 minutes from Christchurch.
There was woodland and beach within walking distance and a couple of other, larger towns I could also walk to.
It was a nice area all around, and the weather was lovely, their summer, our winter, so I went at a good time.

Before Kieran and I embarked on our first, most incredible road trip that he had amazingly planned, we spent New Year's in the family's second home in beautiful Kaikoura.

Kaikoura is 'a little piece of heaven' – Kieran's Mum used to say that, and you couldn't get words more fitting.
Impeccable blue seas, surrounded by majestic snow-capped mountains, and the perfect spot for whale and dolphin watching.
Kaikoura also homes a wonderful seal colony, they bloody stink but are amazing to see.
Some of the walks we went on held the most spectacular views, especially the Peninsula walkway.

All of Kieran's family were already at the seaside home, ready for the celebrations, so this is where I first met them all.
I was bloody nervous, he had a big family, but I soon discovered there was no need to be at all. Everyone instantly treated me like part of the family. They were all so, so lovely and warming.
In all honesty, it felt like I knew them already.

New Year was celebrated with food, drink, and lots of fun.
Kieran took me down to the pier to watch the fireworks, as that's what he likes to do every year, and that's where he told me that 'You will be my wife one day'.
Let's all laugh together.

Our road trip began on New Year's Day.
What a way to start the year.
I had no idea about any of the places we were going to.

It was all one massive, unknown, adventure and I couldn't wait.

Hanmer Springs was our first stop.
Hanmer Springs is best known for the World-famous thermal pools and spa, but I was more interested in all the mountains and tracks I could see.
Hikers' heaven.
Kieran completely treated me here, and we had the most incredible hotel, 'The Braemar lodge'.
I have never stayed anywhere so posh and beautiful.
We had an enormous suite with a double spa bathroom and a private hot tub on the balcony.
It was stunning, as were the views.
I later looked at the cost. fuck me! Nobody has ever spent that much on me.
Kieran always had a way of making me feel so, so special and was always treating me.
I truly felt like a Queen when I was with him.

There are so many walks and day tramps to do in Hanmer.
We did a couple on our first visit, both 'Conical Hill' and the 'Waterfall track'.
Conical Hill was an easy and accessible track but relatively steep towards the end.
The path zig-zagged through exotic forest and woodland until we reached the summit, where there was a cute, wooden lookout shelter.
The 360° views of Hanmer Range, Amuri Range (North), and the Lowry Peaks Range were amazing.

The track up to 'Dog fall waterfall' was just as incredible.

144

Covered by mountain beech trees and surrounded by extraordinary views.

The walk was interesting and varied as it traversed the watershed just above the deep gutter of Dog Stream.

It climbed up wooden stairways in the forest and sidled along small cliff faces to reach the small basin into which the waterfall plummets.

The sounds of the Bellbirds and Tuis filled the air.

I got my first glimpse of the pretty little Fantails too.

I adored these spectacular tiny birds.

I became an avid birdwatcher in NZ. They have the most gorgeous wildlife.

The waterfall was an impressive 41 metres, and we stopped there for lunch and to fill up our water bottles before taking a more challenging track back down into Hanmer.

It was quite amusing as both of us completely underestimated the steepness of the track.

'I don't get it. It looked so flat on the map.'

That evening we had the most delicious and unique meal.

A whole loaf of crusty bread hollowed out and filled with a cheese sauce. It was to die for.

The waistline didn't approve mind, but my taste buds didn't give a crap.

We headed back down South, on a route towards Lake Tekapo, stopping at the most French town in New Zealand, Akaroa.

Filled with its historic buildings, magnificent harbour, and picturesque hills.

Kieran and I embarked on another of our walks and hit the Banks Peninsula.

More incredible views.

NZ must be the most picturesque place in the World.
I'm so glad that we both enjoyed hiking and exploring, just as much as each other.
It was one of our many shared passions.
We also liked playing scrabble, people-watching in coffee shops, and doing arrow words.
Yes, I did say we were both in our 20's at the time, but I agree that reading makes us sound like a couple who could have been born in the 1930s.

The beautiful turquoise blue lake came into view.
The colour is a product of the surrounding glaciers.
The glaciers in the headwaters of Lake Tekapo grind rocks into fine dust on their journey down towards the lake.
The resulting particulate, called 'rock flour,' is suspended in the water and causes the magnificent turquoise colour.
The lake was surrounded by vivid purple lupin.
It was astounding.
I had so many vocal 'Wow' moments on our trip.
I was living the dream.

Kieran told me we would be heading on to Queenstown next.
I'd seen photos of the beautiful, cosmopolitan, Queenstown and I was super excited to be going there.
We had to take an alpine road, the 'Lindis Pass', a mountain pass at an elevation of 971 metres above sea level, linking the Mackenzie Basin with Central Otago.
The road was hilly and winding, with plenty of elevation changes.

The impressive mountains loomed over us, with the yellow snow tussock grassland contrasting against the deep blue sky.

It certainly was an impressive route and so bloody scenic.

Who knew a road could be so picturesque?

I now own a drone called Gimble, and boy, how I wish I owned him while I was in NZ. I would have taken the most epic footage.

Kieran and I had been getting on so, so well.

I loved him a little bit more every day and still couldn't believe that I was in New Zealand, let alone touring the country with him.

A few times, I had to stop and pinch myself.

Queenstown, the 'Adventure Capital of the World', and Lake Wakatipu came into view. I was like a little kid when they spot the sea for the first time.

My eyes completely lit up.

The incredible, enormous lake, which I initially thought was the sea, was surrounded by the dramatic, snowy mountains, and the city streets were bustling with people.

I could feel the energy instantly, and I was buzzing to be part of it.

We stayed at a cute little backpacker's hostel, which was ideal as most of the hikes started nearby.

Our first evening was dream-like.

The sunset was out of this World. Kieran took me on a lakeside stroll, past the pier, and through the tranquil gardens. It was bloody windy, but that didn't matter at all.

I quite liked the windswept photos that were taken of

me.

We sat on the rocks at the edge of the beautiful lake, eating ice cream out of a tub, until the sun had completely disappeared behind the headland.

The pink and orange reflections on the water were mesmerising. Small fishing boats were bopping on the surface, and seagulls circling overhead.

Picture perfect evening.

The following day, we naturally woke up fairly early, grabbed some coffee and croissants for breakfast, and set off to tackle the 'Ben Lomond' track.

The hike began by following the 'Tiki trail', which is commonly known as the 'Queenstown gondola walking track', as it zigzags up the same hill as the gondola goes to reach Bob's peak.

This part of the trial was basically our warmup before hitting the main route and also well used by mountain bikers, so we had to watch our backs.

The trail took us through the dense forest of Douglas firs and into some of Queenstown's most beautiful native beech forests.

I got to see more of those pretty Fantails, along with some Tuis and Woodpigeons.

There were hidden artefacts, including huge wooden chairs, in the forest, which left us feeling like we were in the company of giants.

I looked like a midget when I sat on the mammoth-like chair.

The big scenic reveal at the top was outstanding. The views over Queenstown were unreal, and that was nothing compared to what we would see. We walked to the platform where the Skyline gondola departed, watched a few of the cable cars depart, took some photos, then carried on our hike, trying to ignore the imminent inclines ahead of us.

I'd like to think Kieran and I were both quite fit. We were avid hikers. Well, Kieran did like his pizza. Still, he had started gym training with me, so he was getting fitter anyway, but the 'Ben Lomond' track was tough and challenging, with a steep 1438 metres elevation gain.
The first segment led us through the alpine tussocks and shrubs, with a marked trail contouring alongside the ridgeline.
Followed by magnificent lake and mountain views as we climbed higher up into the saddle.
This is the first time on the hike we got to see the awe-inspiring peaks of 'Mount Aspiring National Park'.
The track continued to get trickier from here.

Beyond the saddle, the path steepened even further and became very difficult.
I stopped at one point and had a childish sulk, 'I can't go any further, my legs hurt, and I'm hungry'.
The summit soon appeared and only seemed to be a few minutes away from where we stood, but the hike from the saddle to the summit took another bloody hour.
I remember crying with laughter. We both looked so messy, sweat running down our faces, both exhausted and completely depleted of energy, yet we carried on.
Neither of us was the type to give up or give in.

A winding, narrow, and exposed trail emerged,

which required some help from our hands for balance.

I didn't fancy doing a rollie pollie down the side of the mountain.

We were both over the moon when we finally reached the summit of 'Ben Lomond', 1748 metres high.

We were rewarded with majestic 360-degree views of Queenstown, the 'Remarkables' ski resort, and 'Mount Aspiring National Park'.

The climb was well worth it, and we earnt our pints and dinner that evening.

A few pints, in fact.

I could have stayed in Queenstown for weeks and weeks, but our time was limited, and it was time for us to mosey on to our next stop.

Wanaka, via Arrowtown.

Arrowtown was a place like no other.

A quaint little gold miners' village, full of history and heritage.

Lined with 19th-century miners' cottages, cafes, shops, and restaurants.

Kieran spotted an open pub, it was Sunday, and before 10 am, so we weren't expecting to be able to get any grub, but we managed to get a delicious full fry up with a side of extra strong coffee.

It was needed and went down far too well.

Bellies full, we walked down the quiet streets until we reached the 'Chinese settlement'.

Chinese gold miners flocked to this area, and in 1874 3,564 Chinese were living in Otago.

In Arrowtown, the Chinese were forced to live in huts along isolated gullies on the banks of Bush Creek at the edge of town.

Many of the huts had been restored, which offered us the chance to step back into that 'golden' era and take some photos.

It was a strange place, but glad we went to experience it.

Ah, where do I even begin with Wanaka?

Striking land formations, soaring mountains, and crystal-clear turquoise lake do not at all do it any justice.

It was a beautiful place.

Wanaka is a place you must visit if you go to the South Island, as is Queenstown... and Hanmer, and Kaikoura, ok fuck it, just go everywhere if you visit, take a year out and do it all!

I got my famous 'Wanaka tree' photos. If you haven't heard of this tree, it is a famous, crocked willow tree that symbolises hope and endurance, it sits alone in the water, and it is one of the most photographed trees in the World.

I believe that this beautiful, symbolic tree was vandalized last year by some wanker who decided to saw some of her branches off.

What is wrong with people?

I really wanted to climb 'Roys Peak', another mountain, but unfortunately, we couldn't stop at Wanaka long, I was gutted I couldn't be in NZ for more than two weeks, but as I had recently started my new job, I couldn't get any more time off.

Kieran had to pack as much as he could into my time there, and that, he definitely did.

Just a few hours later, after an incredibly scenic drive, we were in the car park of 'Franz Josef Glacier' (Kā Roimata ō Hine Hukatere).

It is one of the steepest glaciers in New Zealand, descending from its origins high in the Southern Alps deep into the lush native rainforest of 'Westland's National Park'.

We walked the base path to the foot of the glacier.

A short forest track was followed by a route over shingle and rock, which was uncomfortable and unsteady underfoot.

The glacier was an incredible sight to see.

It was a beautiful yet volatile place.

The warning signs relentlessly reminding us that the glacier was constantly moving and that ice and rock could fall from the terminal face without warning.

It was a magnificent sight, but there were so many tourists there. It didn't feel very special at all. We were all fighting to get the best photos and trying to avoid shots with people's heads in.

I hate tourists, even though I was one of them.

That evening, Kieran and I spent the night at a gorgeous little, secluded B&B, down the road from Franz Josef, in Whataroa.

Whataroa holds the only New Zealand breeding colony of kōtuku (white herons). It sits on the banks of the Waitangiroto River.

I didn't see any of them, though.

That night was one of the most phenomenal evenings of my life.

For the first time, I got to see the milky way.

I can't explain how amazing the night skies were, and I can't explain my emotions. I'd never seen so many stars and so many shooting stars.

I was making wishes every few minutes.

I was so overwhelmed.

I cried at the beauty of it all, and not just a couple of tears either.

We were smack bang in the middle of the 'Aoraki Mackenzie International dark sky reserve'.

There are only 17 dark sky reserves in the whole World.

This one is unique to the Mackenzie Region. The clear skies found in this part of the World are like nothing else in New Zealand.

Very limited light pollution meant the views of the night sky seemed to stretch on as far as the eyes could see.

I will treasure that night forever.

Neither of us could wake up the next morning, so we had a lazy few hours in bed, cuddling, reflecting on the last few days, and drinking coffee.

At this point, we only had a couple of days left on the trip, and I only had a few more days before going home.

It had flown by.

Hokitika, we did quite a bit in this funky little town. Historic Hokitika is a place to appreciate the fascinating history of the West Coast.

A great place to find out about the shipwrecks, gold miners, and pounamu hunters.

Nowadays, Hokitika is known as the 'Cool Little Town'.

We explored the wild West Coast beach, which is famous for its driftwood sculptures.

We strolled along the sand, watched the Tasman Sea's rugged surf, then stopped for a selfie with the famous driftwood Hokitika sign.

Pub lunch, I say pub, it was sort of a café, I'm not sure, but the food was nice anyway.
We then took a short drive to a place we had passed signs for, on the way, the Hokitika Gorge walk.
It was a perfect mini-adventure.
The walking track took us through classic West Coast native bush and over a dubious suspension bridge where we were directly over the incredible turquoise waters of the Hokitika River.
The walk only took around 20 minutes, but it was decent all the same, and I'd recommend doing it.

Next, we took on the spectacular West Coast Treetop Walk.
I loved it.
Wooden walkways are set amongst the native forest canopy of ancient Rimu and Kamahi trees.
We were literally in the treetops surrounded by the songs of the Bellbirds.
Looking down, we could see the spectacular giant ferns from above as we sauntered through the suspended forest canopy walkway.
The Hokitika tower allowed us to climb a further 40 metres above the forest floor and take in the panoramic views of the Southern Alps and the Tasman Sea.
Luckily it was a perfectly sunny day, so we could see for miles.

The time came to head back towards Christchurch.

We took the 'Arthurs Pass' route back.

It is a piece of extreme engineering involving viaducts, bridges, rock shelters, and waterfalls redirected into chutes.

Incredible section of road.

We stopped off at Arthurs Pass village to grab some lunch and have a leg stretch.

We were greeted by a few Keas.

Then we saw a sign for 'Devils Punchbowl walking track'.

Intrigued, we went off wandering to see what it was all about.

After a short walk through some woodland and over Devils Punchbowl creek, we could feel the full force and sound of fresh mountain water falling 131 metres.

One of New Zealand's most stunning waterfalls.

On our little road trip, we covered 1576 kilometres by car and just under 207 kilometres by foot.

Not bad, considering we were away for just over a week.

My last few days were spent exploring local tracks and trails and getting to know the family a bit better.

Kieran had an older sister, who had two beautiful children, and a younger brother, and a gorgeous dog, called Diesel.

I loved that little pooch.

We had already talked about 'what happens next?'.

Kieran was to sort out a short-term visa and come to the UK for a while.

My departure day arrived, and Kieran put stamps on me to post me back home.

'Amy's on her way back home to you.'

Mum received the photos of me with stamps on my

forehead and found it hilarious.

I flew back to the UK and waited to find out about his arrival.

At the end of March 2018, Kieran flew back over to England.
Before he arrived, I had already found us a place to rent, in the beautiful Marlow.
I was working in Reading at the time, still with Thames Valley Police, and you can't get any more perfect than Marlow to live.

Initially, it was awkward between us.
I hadn't seen him in almost four months, and he looked so different.
Honestly, he didn't even look like him. It was like collecting a stranger from the airport.
He had a lot of weight.
He just missed me too much to even eat.

After the first couple of weeks, we were ok again, and thankfully, it would have been extremely horrid if not.
Kieran had a six-month visa, and we also had a six-month tenancy.
I fell in love with living in Marlow, a very classy but extremely friendly place, with many riverside walks.
The walk to Henley was one of my favourites.
There was always something going on as well, and we would be out most evenings at some 'party in the park', boat race, swan upping, festival, or food market.
Very eventful little town.

I took Kieran all over England.
We holidayed in the Peak District and Cornwall, and I also took him up to bonnie, Scotland.
He loved it up there as much as me.
September soon came around, and once again, we had decisions to make.

Being with someone who lives so far away is not the easier of things.
I do not recommend it.
Fall in love with someone that lives down the road, or in the next town, not on the other side of the bloody World.

I decided to get myself a short-term visa and go back to NZ with him.
Nobody had a say in the matter.
I had to give up my job in the police to do so, I loved that job, but I also loved Kieran and New Zealand.
I hadn't considered what I would do for money. I hadn't considered anything, another spur of the moment Amy situation, but still one I certainly do not regret.

It was nice to be doing the stupidly long flight together.
This time our flight path went via Shanghai, Sydney, and Auckland, rather than Dubai and Melbourne.
The airport in Shanghai is insane. You can tell the country has money.
Same as Dubai.
Designer shops, chandeliers, fountains, not your usual basic, duty-free, that's for sure.

My time in NZ was different this time around.

I was living there, rather than being on holiday there.

I applied for endless jobs but was unsuccessful. No one was interested in someone who was only there for a short period.

I tried bar work but hated it, too many sleazy men perving on me, and as I had never pulled a pint in my life, young lads laughing in my face really didn't help either.

I did one shift and called it quits.

At least I tried it, I guess.

I also did some odd jobs and cleaning work for Kieran's family business, then decided to do something mega.

New Zealand is where my own fitness business, 'Girly Green Gym' was initially born.

A big ol' leap to take in a country where I knew nobody, but it worked.

Before coming up with 'GGG', I spent days and days sitting in my favourite little café, 'Coffee Culture', drinking endless amounts of cappuccinos and people watching while brainstorming business ideas and names.

I felt like a right little businesswoman.

Sat at a corner booth with my laptop.

I also went to the local library to research ideas and get lost in books.

I ran my outdoor boot camps in a beautiful park in Rangiora, 'Matawai park'.

It was a perfect open space.

Lots of green areas, but also surrounded by woodland, streams, and a quaint pond home to a family of ducks.

I made friends quickly and loved what I was doing.

Some of the girls I met over there, I stay in touch with now. In fact, I gave one of the girls, Baylee, all my fitness stuff once I left so that she could take over the classes.

Whether she still does them or not, I don't know.

And one lovely lady I met due to GGG, Michelle, has become a true long-distance best friend.

She is one of the most inspiring ladies I have ever met, been through more than you could ever imagine, and come out the other side stronger than ever.

Super proud of her, and I hope to see her again one day.

Kieran's dad let me use one of their vehicles, a little old van called 'Jac'. It saved me a two-hour walk into Rangiora every day.

Jac was a legend.

I signed up to a local gym, 'Snap fitness', as did Kieran, and it was great to be properly training again.

I had a gym in Marlow but was so busy with work that I couldn't go as regularly as I would have liked to.

I started getting back into my yoga as well, and I even got Kieran into it.

We would do a short routine before bed most evenings.

The botanical gardens in Christchurch became my go-to place when I wanted some time to myself or when I just wanted to get lost in all its beauty.

I adored it there.

I spent the morning of my 29th birthday sitting in the café, eating cake, drinking coffee, watching the birds, and admiring the views.

It is a tranquil oasis of colour that covers over 51 acres, and the stunning Avon River meanders its way right through its centre.

There are many different gardens to be explored, including the rose garden, the herb garden, the Asian garden, and the New Zealand garden.

I think there are 25 gardens in total.

The rose garden was one of my most visited.

Set in front of a large greenhouse conservatory, it reminded me of a secret garden.

The gardens also have a variety of different walkways and woodlands.

Beswick's walk is an avenue of lime trees, it smelt amazing while dawdling through it, and it looked beautiful.

There are over 350,000 species of plants within the botanic gardens.

I didn't even know that many existed.

The gardens are also a fantastic place to bird-watch and feed the ducks.

I'd often spot a Silvereye, Fantail, or Redpoll, along with the more common Sparrow, Blackbird, and Chaffinch.

A month or so after being back in NZ, Kieran decided to take me on another road trip, but this time in Jac and further up North.

We headed to Picton, Blenheim, Nelson, and Lewis Pass.

It was epic.

We chucked a mattress in the back, popped curtains on the windows, and added fairy lights around the edges.

He looked adorable.

We washed in rivers and lakes and cooked over a small gas hob.

There is no true feeling of freedom than when you wake up, push open the back door, and instantly look out over the sea.

Not a soul in sight.

We parked up in some awesome places, all with their own unique, incredible views.

You are allowed to 'freedom camp' in New Zealand, so we were always spoilt when choosing where to pitch up.

Why can't we have this in England?

My favourite was a secluded spot on the Ashley River, not sure why. It wasn't the most scenic at all, but I felt most alive there.

Another few places we stopped off at were owned by the department of conservation (DOC).

DOC has basic campsites where you can stay for free and scenic and standard campsites where you are required to pay a charge.

We stayed at one free one, which was a green area overlooking the coast. The other we stayed at was right on the beach.

It was beautiful, very hippy, and colourful, but beautiful.

Kieran had bought me a cute elephant soft toy previously, and I named him Arthur.

He came on all our trips as my little mascot, and he still does come with me on all of mine, even now.

I think he needs to go through the washing machine now, though.

In November 2018, I was extremely fortunate and got invited to the family holiday in Fiji.
Wow.
I couldn't believe it. Fiji.
I couldn't turn down an offer as amazing as that, and I will always be eternally grateful.

'Plantation Island resort', on Malolo Lailai Island.
We had arrived.
After our flight, we had to take a short boat trip across to the Island, where we were greeted on the pontoon with the happier staff I have ever come across, all singing and dancing, and gifted us all beautiful garlands made of frangipani flowers.

The white sands, clear waters, and palm trees were exactly what I had imagined.

It was a tropical, paradise island.

The days were spent lounging on the beach, chilling in the hammocks beneath the coconut trees, exploring the plantations, swimming in the pool, and sipping cocktails at the bar.
Bliss.
I experienced proper snorkelling for the first time, and the underwater wildlife in Fiji is indescribable.
The crystal-clear waters are full of colourful fish, turtles, stingrays, beautiful coral, and lots of sea snakes.
It was surreal to be swimming amongst them all and quite scary at times.
I found out after that some of the snakes I'd seen are

the most poisonous in the World.
Brilliant, and there I was, swimming a foot away, taking photos with my waterproof case.

I, Kieran, Kieran's brother, and his girlfriend all hired bikes for the day and toured the whole island. That was a great day, so much fun.
Twenty-three acres of tropical landscaped gardens, coconut palms, kilometres of white, sandy beaches, and a gorgeous, sheltered lagoon, all explored by pedal power.
I did feel very lucky to be there.
It is a stunning place.

The sunrises and sunsets are like none I have seen before, and I've seen a fair few in my time.
The whole island illuminates with orange and red glows. At the same time, the calm waters reflect the fiery colours and resemble a sheet of tie-dyed silk.
Gratitude like no other was felt each time I watched the sunrise and fall.

The holiday was soon over, and we returned to Kiwi soil.
Christmas was now fast approaching, the streets and shops looked beautifully festive, yet it felt so odd as it was the peak of their summer.
Christmas, for me, is being wrapped up in my scarf and woolly hat, not wandering around in shorts and a strap top.

For some reason, I started to get incredibly homesick.
To the point, I was giving myself anxiety over it and

getting myself extremely upset.

My parents being so far away from me suddenly really got to me, and all I wanted to do was go home.

I wanted to spend Christmas with Kieran and his family, but I also felt such a need to be with my own family.

Maybe because of the whole Jeremy Kyle Canada trip? I honestly don't know, but I couldn't fight the feeling.

Kieran's parents were amazing. They looked after me so much.

They even put on a full Christmas day early, so I could share it all with them before going home.

They were, and are, wonderful people.

That moment at Christchurch airport, saying goodbye to Kieran, was one of the hardest things I've ever done.

I had fallen for him hard, even more so after being back in NZ, and little did I know that that would be the last time I would ever see him.

I arrived back in the cold, wet UK at the start of December 2018, with no idea what I would do next with my life.

I had no home, no job, and no fucks to give.

8 COASTLINES, CLIFFS & CORNISH PASTIES
"Escape and breathe the air of new places."

My Mum and Dad had moved down to Lostwithiel, Cornwall, from Northampton, while I was away.

I had nowhere to call home when I returned, so they had no choice but to let me move in with them.

At this point, Kieran was sorting out his UK residency visa, which could have taken as long as a year to finalise.

He was going to come and live with me in the UK, we talked about getting a place together in Scotland or Cornwall, as we both loved the areas, and we would return to NZ as often as we could afford to do. His parents said they would visit us in England also.

There were no jobs, at all, that I wanted to do in Cornwall.

Indeed, it is usually packed with jobs, but down in Cornwall, nope, nothing.

I considered joining the police, but they weren't recruiting.

I looked for reception and gym jobs, nothing.

So, I ended up working as a retail assistant at 'Trago Mills', which is a massive department store.

Not the best job in the World by any means, and a slight step backwards from everything else I had done, but it was a job, and I could start straight away.

I needed the money.

Once again, I was living in a place where I knew nobody.

The majority of my friends were up Oxfordshire and Lincolnshire way, so the one good thing about working at Trago was that I got to know a few people.

Everyone was lovely, to be honest, and as I started working there a couple of weeks before Christmas, even most of the customers were lovely too.

I worked in a department next to a short girl with pink hair, Kirsty, who is now a good mate.

About a week before Christmas, Kieran seemed off with his calls and texts.

We spoke, every day, as much as we could with the time difference.

His messages seemed short and blunt, not like him at all. He was usually the soppy kind, which I loved.

I questioned it, obviously, that's what we do as females, but he said everything was fine, and he didn't even realise he had been acting differently.

Hmm.

Then just two days before Christmas eve.

166

Yup, Christmas time again.

Always get my heart broken at Christmas time.

A couple of texts, and a phone call, and just like that, it was over between us.

'You deserve a lot better than me, Amy.'

I wasn't having any of it.

I sent essay after essay of how much I loved him but got nothing in return.

He erased me off all social media platforms that same day and then changed his number.

I couldn't understand it at all.

I couldn't understand how I was back in this position. We had had our ups and downs, of course, every couple does, but the good always outweighed the bad, and I knew he loved me.

We had the best adventures together and still share so many memories from so many different parts of the World.

He was a massive part of my life, and if it weren't for meeting him, I never would have explored New Zealand or Fiji, and I would never have created 'GGG'.

So, I have a lot to thank him for, really.

I don't hate him for ending it at all, and I do sometimes still wonder 'What if?' But I know you can't think like that.

I don't know if it could have ever worked anyway, he was close to his family, and I'm close to mine. One of us would have had to give it all up.

As with the ginger, I thought Kieran was the one. I thought I would marry him and have a family with him.

We had a future planned and a bright future at that.

I think I'm destined never to wear a pretty engagement or wedding ring.
My current partner doesn't want to get married.
Boo.

I took the breakup pretty hard and once again used the gym, along with long coastal hikes, as my focus.
I don't cope with heartbreak too well, so fingers crossed I don't have to go through another one, and if I do, don't let it be over the bloody festive season, please.

Despite everything, I did have a lovely first Christmas down in Cornwall, my sister and her now ex-partner came down, and we all spent it together.
Me, Mum, Dad, Anna, Rhys, and both the dogs, Connie and Rambo.
Connie is Mum and Dad's mental Cockapoo, and Rambo was Annas's gorgeous German shepherd.

Cornwall is beautiful, hence why I am still here now, and while I was fixing my shattered little heart, I tried to explore it as much as possible.
On days off, I would take myself out for the whole day. Pack up a picnic and a flask of coffee and drive somewhere new, where I would spend the day hiking and discovering the area.
Usually with sad, depressing music in my ears, which was stupid, really.
Cheers Adele.

I've been down here in Cornwall almost three years

now and still haven't covered even a quarter of it.

One of my favourite places to get lost in is 'Trevose head'.

The sunsets there are unreal, and the coastal path hikes are incredible.

If I am having a crappy day or week, I am instantly made happy again as soon as I pull up in that cliff-top car park.

They say your third love comes when you least expect it.

In February 2019, I met Baz for the first time.

I was at work, strolling up the killer hill to the warehouse, to slay some time and get some fresh air, when one of the delivery vans drove past.

It stopped up ahead of me, and a capped figure jumped out.

'I would have offered you a lift, but it looked like you were enjoying the walk.'

His smile instantly made me smile.

I continued to see him around work, and we exchanged nods and smiles, but that was all.

God, there was something about him, though.

He gave me butterflies, a feeling I hadn't felt in a long time, and I was always looking out for him.

I got asked to be an Easter bunny at a work event, pink tutu, bunny ears, the works.

That's where I first became friends with Jamie, who is now one of my closest friends down here in Cornwall. In fact, I am one of her bridesmaids next year.

I was stood at the stall with Jamie, all bunnified, when a friend request came through on Facebook

It was him. Baz.

My heart was racing.

I accepted, and after a few hesitations, I messaged him.

Fuck it.

I told him to come and see me in my bunny costume.

He did.

After that day, he started coming to find me at work regularly, just to say hello.

Cute.

One time he brought me a big box of Maltesers and gave me a massive, unexpected cuddle.

Chocolate, and hugs, are, without a doubt, the way to my heart.

I was falling for him.

Dam it.

We had both recently come out of serious relationships, and neither of us had been looking for anything at the time, so both agreed to take it slow.

Yeah, that didn't happen.

Baz gave me a key to his place within the first couple of months of seeing each other.

To be fair, I was spending more time there than I was with my parents, so it made sense.

He lived right on the moors, about 30 minutes from my parents, and this is still where we both call home now.

It's not a bad part of the World. In fact, it's rather splendid.

Our first date was like no other.

No usual drink at a bar, no dinner at a fancy

restaurant, no movie at the cinema, oh no, we had the most beautiful sunset walk up the moors, with a flask of coffee.

It was perfect. It was like he knew me already.

I'd chose that over a pub or restaurant any day of the week.

The photos taken that evening are still some of my favourite pictures of Baz.

A few weeks after moving in with him, I found his driving license and almost had a heart attack.

'Aaron', who the fuck was Aaron?

I even rang my sister, 'Oh my God, Anna, I don't even know what his real name is, and I've been seeing him for over two months'.

I didn't even confront him. I was too embarrassed.

Instead, I started asking around at work, but everyone just knew him as 'Baz'.

I later found out that 'Baz' was/is a nickname from his childhood, and indeed his real name is 'Aaron'.

Glad that was all figured out.

I left Trago at the end of summer 2019 for another stop-gap job, but with better pay.

A receptionist at the famous 'Jamaica Inn'.

I quite enjoyed it there, and the majority of the staff were in my age group or younger, and I felt much more at home.

Plus, I got free meals.

I got on well with everyone, as I, weirdly, always seem to everywhere I go.

Not going to lie, about eight months into my relationship with Baz, things got pretty rocky, and we were so up and down.

I thought that we were done.

Alcohol had a lot to do with it. In fact, it had everything to do with it.

It really is the devil at times.

We were both adolescent drinkers.

We had hellish arguments and fights.

Sober, we were head over heels in love with each other, but drunk, we were enemies.

It was vile and unexplainable.

So, in December of that year, when Covid had just started to rear its ugly head, we took a break.

His idea.

Initially, I wasn't best pleased about it, but it was necessary.

We both still wanted to be with one another. Still, we both needed to level ourselves, sort our shit out, and try to understand why we were arguing so much over nothing.

I moved back in with Mum and Dad, then decided to fuck off on holiday, alone.

I booked myself an all-inclusive spa holiday, and then on 26th January 2020, I flew out to Costa Teguise in Lanzarote.

It was bliss and one of the best things I've ever done.

I hugely recommend taking a holiday solo.

I could do whatever I wanted when I wanted.

Oh, and I had a king-size bed all to myself.

I got up early for sunrise walks most mornings, then had the most delicious breakfasts before laying in the sun, sipping cocktails by the pool.

This was usually followed by an hour or twos session in the incredible spa.

It had everything in that spa.

Afternoons were spent exploring the windy coastline or relaxing on the beach. Sometimes, I'd even go back to the spa. It was that good.

I still spoke to Baz every day, and he did call me on a few occasions.

The evenings I spent away did feel quite lonely at times. I missed him a lot.

I went to the entertainment at the hotel and had a few drinks each night, but all the other residents were with a family or a partner.

I was sat there, alone.

Therefore, I tended to take my drinks back to my room and sit on the balcony.

I preferred that.

It was odd seeing Baz for the first time once I got back from holiday.

I hadn't seen him in a good few weeks.

He met me after work one night, we had a drink, and I stayed at his.

He had made an effort, wearing his 'nice' jeans and a shirt, and he was freshly shaved.

It was all still awkward at this point, we weren't together, but we were together.

I didn't really know what was going on.

We both weren't in the right place mentally.

I wanted the relationship to work more than anything. If it weren't for alcohol, we never would have even broken up in the first place.

I hated him drunk, which was more and more frequent, to the point I thought he had a problem, and he hated me drunk. I got angry with him easily, so together, we were always a disaster waiting to happen.

I don't even know why we drank so much together; I rarely drank before moving in with him, only at weekends, but I guess because he liked a drink so much, I sort of just went with it.

Stupid.

Really stupid.

Especially since my past was so messed up because of alcohol.

I didn't move back in properly until March 2020, when the first lockdown happened and when we had had over three months of living apart.

You don't know what you've got till it's gone and all that.

I think we both jumped into the relationship too quickly, and we hadn't had time to even process our previous relationship break-ups, let alone have some time and space to focus on ourselves.

They say you meet your third love when you least expect it and when you aren't looking.

That was definitely the case, but we should have just taken it a lot slower, regardless of how we felt for each other.

Live and learn.

We are now the strongest and happiest we have ever been together and drink very infrequently, and when we do, we are fine, and fingers crossed, it will stay that way.

I love the absolute pants off him. He is my best friend, and he is one of the most loyal, genuine people I know. And despite our past issues, neither one of us ever gave up on each other.

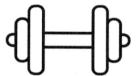

9 TOOK THE PLUNGE & NOW I OWN A BUSINESS

"Our fantasies are our realities in an excuse-free World."

I got furloughed from Jamaica Inn and ended up never going back.

In many ways, for me, lockdown 1.0 was one of the best things that could have happened.

In that time, I became a published children's author and fully launched my own business.

As you've probably gathered, I'm not one to just sit around, lazing in front of the TV, wasting my life away.

You remember Arthur, the soft elephant toy I told you about? Well, he was the main character and the main inspiration for my kids' books.

The books were written about his adventures around the World.

I've currently written four, and they are now selling globally on good old Amazon.

My talents are endless, aren't they!?

You can start with nothing, and out of nothing, and out of no way, a way will be made.

Between writing my books and redecorating the whole house, I thought, 'Why not bring the 'Girly Green Gym' to Cornwall?
So that's exactly what I did, but on a much bigger and better scale.
In NZ, it was really just a way to meet people and get some pocket money, but over here, it was my full-time job and main money earner.
I was determined to make it work, and if I didn't take the opportunity when I did, I probably never would have.
Not everybody supported me at first.
'How stupid to leave a full-time job for something that might not even work?'

Life is about taking risks now and again. It would be pretty boring otherwise.
We need to get out of that comfort zone, and just bloody do it sometimes.
Take that chance. What's the worst that could happen?

I spent days and days advertising and creating social media platforms.
At the time, after lots of research, I found out there were no other outdoor fitness classes at all in the area.
In fact, there weren't any in Cornwall.

'Outdoor boot camps for ladies of all shapes, sizes, and abilities... To commence as soon as lockdown restrictions are lifted.'

In the first couple of weeks, I already had over 300 followers on the Facebook page, and I was bombarded with messages.

I was overwhelmed. Everyone was eager to get fit and to get fit with me.

To keep all my new fans engaged, I started running live workouts for free most days of the week, and I even set up a YouTube channel.

A full gym was set up in the spare room.
Cable machine, treadmill, spin bike, barbells, dumbbells, punch bag, and benches.
A perfect place to run private personal training sessions.
Everything was coming together perfectly.

My first Bootcamp sessions went amazingly.
I had keen ladies in every class, even my 6.30 am.
It was the confidence boost I needed.
I knew it could and would work.
I was initially running five sessions every single day and joining in with them all.
I was pooped.

I now have over 700 people on my page and over 30 personal training clients, and I love them all.
Well, I mean, there are a few bitches, but still, we crack on. They pay me at the end of the day.
Girls, if you're reading, I am joking. I do love you all, but Fiona, cake eating Fiona, you are a pain in the arse, Steph your boobs are too big, they bounce everywhere, Beth you never stop moaning, and for the life of me, I cannot keep up with your love life,

and bloody hell, Sam, well I don't even know where to begin with you mate.

I primarily focus on the PT sessions now, as they are where the money is at, and it's what I enjoy the most.
Plus, I get to be at home every day, so I can eat and drink when I please.
The boot camps run less regularly, but they were, and I guess still are, the bread and butter of my business.
I am extremely proud of myself for building it up from nothing, all by myself, and for meeting so many wonderful women along the way.
I have been told by many that it's not just their physical health that I help, but their mental health too, and for me, that's priceless and so heart-warming to hear.
At times I do feel like I'm more of a counsellor than a personal trainer.
I'm more of an 'all-rounder'.
I'm a fitness instructor, a therapist, a cleaner, a first aider, an agony aunt, and a friend.
You get your money's worth with me, that's for sure.

I celebrated 'GGGs' first anniversary very recently, and I hope to celebrate many more.

I thank everyone that continues to support me, it's not always easy being self-employed, especially with everything that has been happening over the World over the last couple of years, but the girls are always there, which enables me to carry on doing what I do.

10 LIVING THE VAN-TASY
"The biggest adventure you can take, is to live the life of your dreams."

I brought an old Mercedes 308D motorhome and named him 'Manuel'.
Don't ask how we came up with the name.
Another spur-of-the-moment idea, the van and the name, but it suits him well.
I saw him in the marketplace and fell in love, as did Baz, the interior, exterior, everything. Therefore, I had no choice but to buy him.

He is the perfect little home on wheels.
Immaculate living/dining room area furnished with a grey sofa and fox-themed curtains.
Cupboards everywhere.
The kitchen is your bog-standard van kitchen. My favourite thing in there is our blue whistling kettle, and then we have the bedspace above the cab and the bathroom, complete with toilet and shower.
Everything we need.
It took a while to get used to all the buttons and

179

switches and 'servicing' him.

Filling the water tank, checking the gas, emptying the grey waste... emptying the loo... all delightful, regular tasks that have now just become routine.

I have always wanted a van, to be fair, but I didn't think I would own one this soon.

I had savings in the bank, and then my beloved Nan passed away in February 2021 due to Covid and left me some money.

Another very upsetting event that hit the family hard, especially, and understandably, my dad, Uncle, and Aunt.

My Nan lives on and shares adventures with me in Manuel.

She loved Italy and Spain and red wine. My intentions are to take Manuel over to Europe once we are free to roam the World a bit more freely again.

Then we will sit in the sun with a glass of red and raise a toast to my Nanny.

Baz and I have already had lots of trips in the van. He is my happy place. Honestly, when I wake up in Manuel, my life feels worry and stress-free. It's an amazing feeling.

Away from the daily grind, away from housework, away from the monotonous routine, away from the hustle and bustle.

I just feel free.

We have woken up in some beautiful locations, most of them are coastal, but some on moorland, some high up with 360° views, and some just in car parks.

It doesn't matter where we go. The excitement still exists.

We recently went away for a few nights, only to Devon, but it was probably our best little staycation yet.

We pitched up in a beautiful spot overlooking Plymouth Sound. The beach was just a short walk away, the coastal path was also within walking distance, and there was a local pub and shop.

The weather was perfect.

As was our first day, we went swimming in the clear waters of Bovisands, had a BBQ dinner on the beach, had a few bevvies, ok a lot of bevvies, in the sun, then chilled out with cuddles, on our super comfy sofa, while watching a movie.

I can see how people live in a van full time, and I'd be lying if I said we haven't thought about it.

There are minimal bills to worry about, different views every day, and you can take your 'home' wherever you want to go.

To me, van life represents freedom, travel, adventure, and minimalism.

It is a way of life and a means of living more in harmony with yourself.

It's about taking each day as it comes and living life in the unknown to pursue what makes you feel most alive.

It's about making friends with strangers and being part of a nomadic community.

Van life does involve living in a van, yes, and yes, there is often travel involved.

But deeper than that, it is about the commitment to create the most fulfilling, exciting life you can for yourself.

It's about not settling for all the 'shoulds' that others try to push upon you.

It's about focusing on what's meaningful in your life and discarding what isn't.

It's about creating your path and travelling down that path.

Who knows what's to come, and maybe, one day, we will end up living in Manuel at some point.

There's so much I want to do, and unfortunately can't do it all at once.

I'll be 32 by the time this book is published. Ideally, I would like to start a little family over the next couple of years and have a cute little adventure baby, which would mean getting a bigger place to live or converting what we have. Still, I also want to hike the 'Te Araroa' trail in New Zealand, which could take up to six months, and I also want to travel Europe in Manuel, and road trip around Scotland, and want, want, want, want, want.

I always want more, even when I have everything. That's just me.

I probably will end up doing all of it as well. To be honest, the hardest thing out of all of the above, other than the financial part, is the baby component, as that sort of needs two people to commit, and I don't think the other half is quite there yet.

He won't even let me get a dog right now, I can't persuade him to let me have that, so I'm going to have to be on my best behaviour for a long, long time for him to allow me to get preggers. Still, the ol' body clock is ticking away, so, no pressure Baz.

Until we decide what we will do in the future, we

will continue to roam the UK in our trusty Merc, continue to work hard and enjoy our lives together in every way that we can.

And readers, there's no big mystery about doing and achieving everything that you want.
If you want something badly enough, and decide that you will get it, then you will. You need to remember that you can do it, and you can do it with anything in your life.
There are people in all situations and circumstances living the kind of life others dream of, that you dream of, who aren't necessarily talented, rich, or fabulous, but the key to their success is that they just decided to go for it. They stopped listening to their lousy excuses and got the fuck on with it, and you can too.
Just do it.

AUTHOR NOTE

Thank you so much for reading 'Should, Would, Could, Did'.

I hope you've enjoyed reading this book as much as I have enjoyed writing it.

Huge insight into my life.

I'm not a writer by any means, and I have completed the whole book process completely solo.

I even designed the front cover myself.

I would appreciate it if you could pop back on to Amazon and leave me a review, it's a huge boost to independently published authors, like little old me, plus I like people bigging me up.

ABOUT THE AUTHOR

Amy Coutin is a very inspirational woman.

Described by many as 'a ray of sunshine', with her infectious smile and contagious laugh, she is guaranteed to brighten up even the darkest of days, whether you know her or not.

She is a go-getter, a life lover, and hugely motivated and determined to achieve anything she sets her mind to.

Amy has achieved an immense amount and tackled a huge sum of obstacles along the way.

Not only does she motivate people for a living, but she motivates others just by her sheer strength and courage to never, ever give up, even when things get tough.

Being an ex-member of the male-dominated RAF fire service, she will always be 'one of the lads'.

Her passion for the outdoors and adventure is what has enabled her to write these pages and share her stories with the World.

Printed in Great Britain
by Amazon

74021717R00112